I Want to Destroy Myself

A Memoir

MALIKA AMAR SHAIKH

Translated from the Marathi
by JERRY PINTO

SPEAKING
TIGER

SPEAKING TIGER BOOKS LLP
125A Ground Floor, Shahpur Jat,
New Delhi–110049, India

First published in India in hardback by Speaking Tiger 2016
This paperback edition first published in 2023

ISBN: 978-93-5447-434-7
eISBN: 978-93-86050-98-4

10 9 8 7 6 5 4 3 2 1

Typeset in Minion Pro by SŪRYA, New Delhi
Printed at Chaman Enterprises, New Delhi

Malika Amar Shaikh is an acclaimed Marathi poet, novelist and non-fiction writer. Other than her memoir, *Mala Uddhvasta Vhaychay*, her published work includes books of poetry: *Valucha Priyakar* (*A Lover Made of Sand*), *Mahanagar* (*Metropolis*), *Deharutu* (*Seasons of the Body*) and *Manuspanacha Bhinga Badalyavar (When the Lens of Being Human Changes*); works of fiction: *Ek Hota Undir* (*There Was Once a Mouse*), *Koham Koham?* (*Who Am I?*), *Handle with Care* and *Jhadpanachi Ghosht* (*The Story of a Tree*); and a biography of her father, Shahir Amar Shaikh, *Sura Eka Vadalacha* (*The Song of a Storm*).

Jerry Pinto is a writer and poet based in Mumbai. His books include the novels *Em and the Big Hoom*, *Murder in Mahim* and *The Education of Yuri*; the non-fiction book *Helen*; and two books of poetry, *I Want a Poem and Other Poems* and *Asylum*. He has also published landmark translations from Marathi and Hindi, among them: Baburao Bagul's classic story collection *Jevha Mi Jaat Chorli Hoti* (translated as *When I Hid My Caste*); Sachin Kundalkar's novel *Cobalt Blue*; and the memoirs of Daya Pawar (*Baluta*), Malika Amar Shaikh (*I Want to Destroy Myself*), Eknath Awad (*Strike a Blow to Change the World*) and Swadesh Deepak (*I Have Not Seen Mandu*). In 2016, Jerry Pinto received the Windham-Campbell Prize and the Sahitya Akademi Award.

'Malika Amar Shaikh's incredible memoir...is not a book you can move on from...[It] leaves out nothing: you see Shaikh hit puberty; have sex for the first time; have an episiotomy in a filthy hospital during the nightmare of delivering her child... You see the emotional battles between her and Dhasal, her own bad behaviour as well as his, the freezing of their marriage when you realise, along with Shaikh, that she isn't seen as an equal, and the blows, the fights, the suicide attempts. And you see a political consciousness forming...a tragic, first-hand understanding of where women stand even among ideologues who claim to understand egalitarianism, whose hearts bleed for the poor and marginalised but never for the women in their homes whose physical and emotional labour they demand as their right.'—*The Ladies Finger*

'[Shaikh] doesn't demand pity or sympathy by weaving out the fabric of her abusive marriage; she doesn't shy away from speaking her mind, from criticising her husband, Namdeo Dhasal, founder of the Dalit Panthers, meant to fight caste discrimination. And most importantly, she is unafraid to be unabashedly herself even if her opinions seem controversial... Her memoir holds importance for asking the most basic questions about women's rights and women's writing, questions lost in the inertia of debates.'—*Feminism in India*

'[Malika's] searing autobiography...is quite a story — poet falls in love with poet and disintegration follows. Malika tears her marriage into shreds with utmost candour...Pinto's translation captures the vivid bitterness of the original. Those interested in Marathi poetry will certainly read the book but it has a wider audience — lying in wait are all those women who wonder why they conform to patriarchal ways and how love can suddenly explode into rage.'—*Civil Society*

To Jenny Marx,
who seemed to be as tall and impossible to ignore
as Marxism itself.

Translator's Introduction

I had heard of *Mala Uddhvasta Vhaychay* by Malika Amar Shaikh but I had not read it. In fact, it seemed to be one of those books that blazed across the sky like a comet and if you were lucky enough to be looking its way, you got a glimpse of it but if you tried to seek it out later, only the void stared back at you.

The book came out to near-universal acclaim. There was as much praise as sympathy for the story of a young woman who had fallen in love, married right out of the schoolroom, and then found herself in the middle of a tempestuous marriage to a political figure who could never be accused of consistency. But once the first print run was over, the book vanished.

I assumed that the Asiatic Society would have it, being a depository library, but their copy was missing too. I tried second-hand book shops and then I managed to run it down with a friend. Mithila Phadke was my student at the Social Communications Media department at the Sophia Polytechnic. The annual magazine was being discussed and Phadke said she would like to interview the author of a book she had just read. The book was, of course, *Mala Uddhvasta Vhaychay*. I had heard that the lady was a recluse, that she didn't open up and I knew the book to be unavailable. Phadke, intrepid journalist in the making, said that her mother knew Prerna Barve nee Shaikh; that she would find a copy and would set up the interview. And so it came to pass that I read *Mala Uddhvasta Vhaychay* many years ago. I was then a slow reader of any script other than the Roman—I still am—but this was a book I could not put down.

Malika Amar Shaikh's tone is conversational but what she is telling you about straddles the personal and the political, the intimate and the public, the bedroom and the venereal disease clinic. As the daughter of one of the most charismatic of lok shahirs—folk poet is such a pale descriptor for these men and their electrifying messages that still make governments queasy and big business downright nauseous—she met the great and the good of both the Communist movement and the experimental theatre. The dramaturge, Anna Bhau Sathe, turns up and so does Bhakti Barve. There are casual references to painters and poets and sculptors but this is not namedropping. Malika Amar Shaikh is describing the Garden of Eden that was her childhood. Here no tears flowed—for the doctors had asked her parents to try and prevent her from shedding tears until the time she was fourteen.

And then Namdeo Dhasal walked into her life.

It seems to have been love at first sight for both of them. It seems to have been a destructive relationship for Malika. It seems to have been a marriage that ended only when Dhasal died in 2014. And so if you are looking for an easy book about a failed marriage, a misery memoir that ends when the woman walks out of the house into the sunshine outside, or even for Nora rejecting the constraints of the doll house, you will not find it here.

What you will find however is an almost unbelievably honest voice. When Malika Amar Shaikh confesses to suicide attempts when she is pregnant, when she tells you of how she sees Smita Patil's roles as the ones she was fated to play, when she tells you of all the courses she tried to take and all the times she simply could not finish what she had begun, you begin to feel uncomfortable. 'Should she be telling me this?' you wonder. 'It's not precisely designed to make me think well of her.'

This then is that rare self-portrait, the one in which you see the warts. It is the story of a marriage. It reminds you of the time when women who sued for divorce were almost sure to lose their children. Leela Naidu, whose autobiography I co-wrote, lost hers. It is the story of a time when the city of Mumbai was beginning to change from being mill-run and mill-led to being what it is today. It is also the story of a woman struggling to express herself.

It is customary to say that one has enjoyed the process. I did not enjoy translating *Mala Uddhvasta Vhaychay*. It would often leave me feeling somewhat in danger of collapse. There is a section in which Malika Amar Shaikh, not yet twenty, finds herself with a baby in a rented room in Lonavla. She has no household help. Her only companion is a male chauvinist who, as an Ambedkarite has probably followed Dr Babasaheb Ambedkar into Buddhism, but cannot help quoting Hindu scripture at Malika. Her husband vanishes for days at a time, haring off to Pune and leaving her alone. She must wash and clean and tend to her baby and fight with the scripture-quoting Mahar.

And then she discovers that her husband has infected her with a venereal disease.

She has no money for treatment and so she bears with it until she is falling over from the weakness and the fevers. There are boils all over her groin.

Finally, she borrows some money.

From a comrade, a woman who worked as a railway-station sweeper.

I read this section and I wept for the young woman with the endless meals and floors and nappies, for the boils and also for the kindness of strangers.

It's that kind of book.

Jerry Pinto

Introduction

To confront your life is sometimes easier than opening it in all its nakedness before others. Many famous, successful, capable men have written autobiographies… but does an autobiography really present a person to others? When, as an ordinary woman, I decided to throw open the doors and windows of my life, I knew I might be accused of stupidity or whatever else but sometimes narratives happen so inevitably that it does not even seem to matter whether there is a reader or not. The story takes shape as of itself.

As a woman I seek justice in a patriarchal world. My role is clear to me.

I have peeled away the skin of my life and served it up to you. Some may say this fruit is inedible but that doesn't matter. It is more important for me to present this very different world of experience in which I have lived, telling the story from my point of view and from the point of view of all women who have been exploited.

As long as women will not put off the garment of shame and inhibition and tolerant self-sacrifice, as long as people ignore women's sufferings and their experiences or take them for granted, as long as women are only adored or pitied, we will all develop the habit of seeing women as victims. And we will take her oppression as a given.

I met so many people, their lives fragmented, wounded. Some stood tall and some were stunted. I met people who were experts at taking advantage of others. But each one of them enriched me in some way, gave me something. In the end, your humanity is constructed of all these experiences but it is up to you to make meaning out of it. At the end of one's life, will it be possible for one to look back with courage?

What does love mean truly?
Is it a tunnel? A vacuum?
Are we at its mouth?
Is there light at the end?
And a long dark frozen road leading to it?

Did my lover go by this road?
How does he look?
Does love that is requited and love that is not
Look the same?

Is love like a bear
That will tickle you to death?[1]
Whose complete form turns up only in dreams?
You catch glimpses in reality: a mane here
A tail there.
His tantrums here.
His wet eyes there.
Or sometimes just that Ashwamedhi[2] smile.

Love: a mirror made of leather
In which one's reflection is horrifying.
Love: sometimes a piece of bread.
Love: sometimes an empty canvas.
Love: a drop of blood secreted by the body
Once outside, it no longer belongs to you.
Love: all the wisdom earned in the struggle

---

[1]This refers to the belief that a bear does not tear you apart but tickles you to death.

[2]The Ashwamedha yagna was led by a horse, followed by an army. The horse wandered and whichever kingdom it set foot in, the king was either called upon to fight or surrender. You had to be pretty sure of yourself to start an Ashwamedha yagna. What an ashwamedhi smile is may be construed from this.

Or a calculation of victory and defeat.
What does one achieve from this?
Once in a while, an Ashoka or a
Napoleon Bonaparte comes along
Who loves himself so well
Or who knows only how to love.
Their unparalleled sacrifice: to love.

Is love just an uncontrolled emotion?
An experience?
The thrum of a soul deep in meditation?
Or a butterfly born of the blood
Which will ever elude capture?

Pain hardens
The once-playful mind.
Isn't love at the root of it all?
A life once stalled
Stops in fear of death.
What does that mean?

Is it only the pain of the passion of life or something else?
Is it a small lamp
That won't let you use your body as wick?
The flame will not catch
And yet it burns your life away.
And yet we can love love
Where does such love come from?
I don't know. I don't know.

Malika Amar Shaikh

1

Bhai[3] was from Barshi.[4] He was born into a Muslim family. His mother's name was Manerbi. His father had abandoned them. As so many other mothers have, Manerbi raised her children working in the fields. Bhai

[3]Bhai refers to Amar Shaikh (1916-1969), the legendary shahir or folk singer of revolutionary anthems. It is difficult to conjure up now what a magnificent and commanding presence he was, but his presence on the dais meant thousands would turn up to listen to him sing.

[4]Barshi is a town in the Sholapur district of western Maharashtra. It is seen as the gateway to the Marathwada region. At the time Amar Shaikh was there, it had three cotton mills.

grew up listening to the rhythm of those timeless ovis, songs set to the rhythm of the manual labour that women do. His first job was that of a cleaner. As a patriotic, progressive young man, Bhai joined the Barshi Trade Union Movement, his first encounter with the red flag, the Lalbaotaas, the Communist Party was then known as before it split up. Since he had a good voice, he would give it a regular workout. His riyaaz was to sing at a high pitch, in the wilds, in the open. He did get a job in a mill but he lost that because of inflation. Then a strike and its attendant arguments, a chance to lead it and a spell in Visapur Jail. It was there that he met his guru Comrade [Raghunath] Karhadkar[5] and was initiated into Marxist thought. Now his life took an unexpected turn. When he was released from jail, he threw himself into working with the Communist Party. He made good use of his strong, tuneful and full-throated voice. Then the Communist Party was banned.[6] Eluding the police dragnet, Bhai went to Kolhapur. There he got a job at

---

[5]Comrade Raghunath Karhadkar, who died in 1980, went to Fergusson College, Pune, where he became a student activist. He joined the Communist Party of India in 1931. In Sholapur, where he was stationed, he participated in many strikes and often went underground. He worked in many areas of rural Maharashtra and wrote a column for *Yugantar*.

[6]The British colonial authorities banned all Communist activity in the 1920s.

Master Vinayak's studio.[7] Here too he found a group of comrades. It was this group that changed his name from Mehboob Patel to Amar Shaikh. But the world of cinema could not hold him for long.

Around this time too, a fabulous love story began: Bhai and Aai. Both were Communist Party workers. They met at a public meeting and soon got to know each other.

Aai was a typical Pathare-Prabhu.[8] She came from a family of five: two other sisters and two brothers. Her name was Kusum Jaykar. In those days, an inter-caste marriage was the stuff of society's nightmares. The greatest uproar happened in Aai's home.

But even before that, the Party decided to oppose their marriage. That was it. They were shattered. Both were committed Party workers who had faith in the Party. However the Party was not sure that the marriage could work, ideologically. Aai was a middle-class woman, well-educated, a graduate. Additionally, she had a job as a clerk

---

[7]Vinayak Damodar Karnataki (1906-1947) was a film director and actor of the 1930s and 1940s. His daughter was Nanda, also a film star. He co-founded Hans Pictures and directed the Marathi film *Brahmachari* which caused a storm when its heroine appeared in a swimsuit.

[8]The Pathare-Prabhus are among the original residents of the city of Bombay. They trace their lineage through Asvapati and thence to Rama and Prithu. But cursed by Bhrigu, they were reduced to being the scribes and scholars instead of the rulers.

in the Municipal Corporation. Bhai was only a 'final-pass' worker. It was clear that they would not suit each other. And this might mean a problem in the working of the Party. Naturally, the marriage was forbidden by Party mandate.

But that wasn't the only opposition. Aai was in the office one day when a total stranger, a Pathare-Prabhu, came to meet her. He offered to adopt her or to give her money. Anything to stop her from marrying a Muslim.

Eventually Rajni Patel intervened. And once the Party had given its permission, who cared about society or indeed the family? Inspired by stories of true love, Aai ran away from home. Her parents wrote her a letter: 'Feed us poison and lay out our bodies and then get married.'

Aai was not the kind to be swayed by this. That generation was strong-willed enough to treat opposition as encouragement and so they managed to get married on a budget of five rupees. 'The registrar looked like he'd been forced to drink a draught of castor oil,' Aai said.

Of course they were poor. And then Prerna came along—Didi, my elder sister. Two boys died in the seventh month. The inadequate food that had to be gulped, the pickets that had to be manned, the ladders to be scaled, the worry of vigils when Bhai was in jail… there wasn't even enough money sometimes to buy milk for the baby.

They had a man to help them around the house. But

when there was no money, how was he to be paid? Aai told him to go back to the village but he refused. He said, 'I don't want money. Give me a piece of bhakri when you have one. If you're going to the *hapees* and Bhai's in the lock-up, who's going to see to the baby?

It is difficult to imagine such humanity.

And then I came along.

I was a sickly child but one who had a tenacious hold on life. Bhai's jail yatra had just ended. Our economic conditions began to get better. He had founded a group called Nayayug Kalapathak. The Communist Party work was on in full swing. Bhai's voice was appreciated at programmes and was always greeted with waves of enthusiastic applause. Even the paid hecklers would be silenced. They would come to disrupt things and would be caught up in the magic of his music, made even more meaningful by its social messages. It was not unusual for two or three lakh people to gather to hear him sing.

When I was three months old, I contracted pleurisy. I hovered between life and death. A course of ninety injections saved my life. But the doctors warned my parents: she must not cry until she is fourteen years old.[9]

---

[9]It was believed that crying needed a deeper inhalation of breath and so the infection would be driven deeper into the lungs. This is from the 'Lecture on the Diseases of Children', *Provincial Medical & Surgical Journal* (1844-1852), Vol. 15, No. 14 (9 July 1851), pp. 370-372.

But I generally did not have the energy to cry. I was the youngest and sick as well so I was coddled with as much care as one takes of a blister on one's palm. And I needed a great deal of taking care of. Diphtheria? Three bouts. Typhoid. A tonsillectomy. Colds, coughs, a parade of childhood diseases. Each month I spent fifteen days in bed, silent, saying nothing. I do not remember feeling hunger.

Because of these diseases, because of this weakness, because I was pampered and because of all the reading I did when I lay in bed, I began to live in a different world, a dream world. Inside my cocoon, I developed into a lonely, stubborn, sensitive girl. I did not know where I began and my cocoon ended. I seem to have been aware that I was spinning it and withdrawing into it at the same time; that its threads were running deep, into my bloodstream.

I remember feverish nights when I would lie on my father's shoulder or in my mother's lap, my eyes closed in exhaustion, my body limp with defeat. My eyes would refuse to open even to look out of the window that was right next to my bed. Here was a pinkish-red staircase, and a small piece of sky and the white fairies of delirium and the handsome prince who would visit me and laugh with me and tease me.

I would drive myself crazy in my imagination, with my imagination.

Reality would be somewhat different.

2

Our area, Saat Rasta, was like a museum of humanity. Earlier we had been in the Municipal Quarters in front of Rani Bagh.[10] I still remember that home and our time in it. Aai gave up her job to look after me. So the Party found us a home in Saat Rasta. It was a place where people of all religions and castes lived together amicably. From time to time, they did uphold the noble traditions of the Great Indian Project and dutifully indulged in some quarrels.

[10]This refers to the zoological gardens at Byculla. They were once called Victoria Gardens and then later renamed, after Independence, the Jijamata Udyan, after the mother of Shivaji. The name Rani Bagh, The Queen's Garden, could apply as well to both women.

The houses were big. They were well-constructed in the old style of building.

In the first few years, we were very poor. When Kalapathak settled down, Bhai started to travel. I was still very ill. But our economic conditions began to improve. Thanks to the efforts of Comrade Dange,[11] Bhai made a couple of trips to the USSR and Czechoslovakia. That was when I was in hospital with diphtheria. Bhai got off the plane and came straight to the hospital. He brought me a whole lot of toys. There were new things in the house now. Every wish of mine was granted.

When I was ill, Bhai bought me a doll that cost fifty rupees. I have never seen a doll like that one. He also bought me storybooks—Tarzan, Vikram and Betaal, the fairy tales of Hans Christian Andersen. I had my own dolls' cooking set. Out of these materials, I constructed another world and slipped into it. After this, we were never deprived of anything.

Bhai called me Chindyadevi—the goddess of rags—because of my obsession with collecting bits of cloth. But the creation of this small hillock of cloth was just one of the many things I got up to. If my dolls were to get married, they had to have small garlands of flowers

---

[11]Comrade Shripad Amrit Dange (1899-1991) was a founding member of the Communist Party of India, editor of the *Socialist*, a newspaper that he founded, and chairman of the CPI until 1978. He also participated in the formation of the state of Maharashtra.

made for them and then we had a marriage procession that would wend its way through the neighbourhood. These were the materials of my cocoon.

I was good at academics. Mathematics, however, was my Enemy Number One. (Still is.) I bunked school regularly because of my various childhood illnesses. Every morning there would be rehearsals at home, of vags[12] and songs. When a vag was being rehearsed, I could prompt without even looking at the lyrics. Didi would dance when the radio began to play, a habit she developed in childhood. I learned by watching her. Because of the eight-year gap between us, we did not fight and beat each other and sulk as other sisters do. I knew too that the atmosphere of our house was different from that of others. Bhai had never finished his education; Aai was a graduate. She had a degree in the humanities. They never fought in front of us. But when was Bhai ever at home? His tours lasted two or three months at a time. It was only during the monsoon that he was with us.

~

I loved the rain. I loved the idea of something pouring down, giving itself so completely. The rain intoxicated me, part of my love of nature. Bhai and Aai would chat and

---

[12]A vag was a playlet or a skit with a message, which sometimes came before a longer performance.

catch up, Didi's laughter would ring through the house and there she would be, dancing. The sky would lower and glower and then the rain would come thundering down. Bhai would put an easy chair in the gallery and sit there. He too loved the rain. Aai would serve tea, the steam would rise from the cup, the rain-chilled breeze would blow, a faint spray would make its way to where I was sitting with a comic book for company…

This was Paradise.

~

Bhai had a special place of his own in the neighbourhood. Our home was seen as the ideal home. People looked at us with respect, yes, with love even. Bhai would be called upon to adjudicate on household quarrels in the chawl.

Sometimes Babu, the grocer, would need an application written for him. Sometimes our neighbour Bali would need a note. Or the Shivaji Mandal would need his signature. Baban had beaten someone up. Or Genya's mother would come in tears to complain about her son beating someone up. Bhai's role was to stop the trouble, dry their eyes, explain things to them. I remember being told of one Krishna who had to be prevented from going off to kill himself because his parents were not getting him married. That married people should contemplate suicide seems ordinary enough; almost natural one might say. But how odd to think that someone might want to commit suicide on account of being single.

~

To Aai, cooking was an ordeal. You could never be sure that there'd be something to eat when you were hungry. And if she were reading a book, we could just forget about food. She wasn't going into the kitchen until she had finished. And then she might just lay the book aside and say, 'Oh, order some food please.' Didi and Aai did not get along. They fought regularly; heated words and assorted melodrama. This meant that I have never had much idea of what good home-cooked food means. Our staple diet was rice, dal and veggies. If we got hungry in the afternoon, it was bread soaked in milk or tea and biscuits. Fearing that I might fall ill, Aai would not give me anything interesting to eat. I would get bored of these insipid and incomplete meals. Kalapathak had assigned a room to Mama and Kesarbai. It was next to ours but self-contained. I would slip off there and Akka—Kesarbai—would ask: 'Have a bite?'

I would be ready in a second. 'Close the door, Akka. And don't tell Aai I ate here,' I would say.

Akka would laugh until her jaws ached.

~

At around this time, a Bengali couple came to live there. She was Sachin Shanker's niece.[13] We called her Didi.

Her husband was Subal Sarkar.[14] Both were excellent dancers. They had been living far away, at Nalla Sopara. This was my first experience of Bengali people. They seemed like an ideal couple. She was well built with plump lips. When she was dancing she would lose herself in the joy of movement. Although her pregnancy was well advanced—she was in her ninth month—she would wrap up her stomach and dance. Both of them were gentle, kind and emotional. They were totally sincere in their work, just the kind of people Bhai loved.

They directed a spectacular dance drama called *Mazha Gaon* (My Village). I remember it clearly. First, darkness in which a beautiful light would issue forth. Then the death of the krauncha bird—the demoiselle crane—and we would move to the present with its

---

[13]Sachin Shanker (1924-2005) was cousin to Uday Shanker and was one of the foremost exponents of what was called dance ballet. He graduated from Uday Shanker's dance studio at Almora with Kameshwar (later Zohra Sehgal's husband) and Guru Dutt and was associated with the Indian People's Theatre Association (IPTA).

[14]Subal Sarkar (1935-2011), who came to Mumbai via Kolkata and East Bengal, was a choreographer of note who worked in more than a hundred films. Many of these were Marathi films and several were with the legendary Dada Kondke. He was also part of the Samyukta Maharashtra movement.

cunning contractors who exploit farmers while filling their own pockets, the moneylenders who charge usurious rates. Then the birds would dance again.

I loved that programme and enjoyed it thoroughly. I went for all the programmes in Mumbai. In the night, someone would hoist my sleeping form up and take me home. I would often see programmes again and again until I knew the lines by heart, until I knew the lyrics of every song. But I was never bored.

Only when Bhai began to sing his Shivaji powada[15] and the 'Garja Jayjaykar' (Roar out the victory) I would run out of the theatre. I couldn't listen to those. While singing these songs, Bhai would be overcome by emotion. He sang with every inch of his being. The veins in his neck would stand out. When he sang the upper note, it would reach into your chest and clutch at your heart. In his powerful voice, those tunes had an electrifying effect. As he essayed the anguish of these great men, he would choke with tears and his listeners would be filled with an understanding of what goes into the making of the hero.

I write all this now but at the time, as soon as I heard the first notes, I would be unable to bear it any longer. My heart would pound, tears would spring from my eyes and I would lose such emotional balance as I had.

---

[15]A powada is a ballad in which the bard tells of heroic deeds. The form is said to have originated in the seventeenth century in Maharashtra to tell the tales of Shivaji Maharaj's exploits.

The excitement of the programme, the confusion backstage, the hurry and the scurry…Bhai's face, tired but contented…Aai's face, concerned…Didi laughing with the group…hands busy tying ghunghroos…faces shining with sweat. I would lose myself in this world, plunging deep into it, past the stage and the audiences, the aficionados and the actors, the applause that would break out when Bhai's powerful voice had succeeded once more in uplifting and inspiring them. This was my life. Here I drew breath and it was a free, happy breath.

In 1962, Bhai acted in the film *Prapanch*.[16] I was sitting in Bhai's lap and watching the film. In one scene Bhai climbs a mountain to kill himself and I screamed out loud, 'Bhai, Bhai, don't go there.'

And then I began to cry.

Everyone looked around.

'Here I am,' Bhai said. 'Look, you're sitting on my lap, love.'

Finally I had to be taken out of the theatre.

Bhai did not sing a single song for the film. His role lasted up to the interval. But for his acting alone, he won a State Award. He acted in two or three films after that

[16]Directed by Madhukar Pathak, this film won the third-best film at the National Film Awards that year.

but they were all left incomplete. After that Bhai refused all offers and focussed only on Kalapathak.

He had a good physique, a fine voice and a face with powerful lines, all of which were good for cinema. He was also a good actor and with the right break, he might have gone far but he refused to follow this will 'o' the wisp. He did not see cinema as a living form. To him, the essence of his work was to perform in a maidan in front of thousands of farmers or workers, to sing for them in his full-throated voice, to entertain them, to make them aware of their rights.

He was fastidious in his choices. He had a refined taste in everything. He wore an immaculate white dhotar and cream sadra. His curly hair stood straight up, as if in imitation of how he held himself. His mouth was a thin, straight line. Over his big brown eyes, which were sensitive and transparent, he wore spectacles with a delicate golden frame. On his shoulder, an axe.

When he was at home, he wore mojdis. He was at his best in a sherwani and churidhar; he looked every inch the Lucknawi nawab. With a dab of attar and the mojdis, the look was complete. Then someone said, 'You don't look like a shahir in that outfit.' Not look like a singer of revolutionary ballads that stirred the people? Bhai never wore those clothes again.

The house was filled with expensive furniture: a couch, a sofa set, curtains, an iron four-poster bed, a deerskin and a lion's skin. There were beautiful things bought in far-flung places. In the showcases, jars and statues bought in distant lands.

Once someone came up to Bhai after a programme. He had been completely enthralled. He was a jeweller. He opened a flat bag and showed the contents to Bhai.

'I have never heard such a wonderful programme before,' he said and asked Bhai to choose whichever stone he wanted. The bag was filled with rare precious stones. Bhai chose a light-green longish one and had it set in a ring. He wore it until the day he died.

Then Aai lost it somewhere.

~

I was seven when I wrote my first poem:

Hirve, hirve gawat, phule bhovti jamat
Jaate mi, maaghaari yete mi…ramat, gamat
(In the green green foliage, the flowers dance
There will I follow, there will I prance.)

That was my first attempt at drawing poetic breath, the first dream that my young mind could turn into words.

As soon as I could read, I began with Bhai's poems. There would be mehfils at home, where poets like Vinda Karandikar, Narayan Surve, Shri Na Pendse would gather and read, exchanging views and opinions. Bhai read poetry beautifully. He believed that just as one poured one's heart and soul into the writing of a poem, one had to pour out one's essence into the reading of it so that it might be absorbed by the listener.

After Bhai's work, I was drawn to Kusumagraj's poems. I would read them again and again, memorizing them. And if we had visitors, it was I whom Bhai would call upon to recite:

> *Yugamaguni challi re, yuge hi*
> *Karavi kiti, Bhaskara, vanchana*
> *Kiti kaal kakshet dhavu tuzhya mi*
> *Kitida karoo preetichi yaachna*
>
> (Age follows age and yet you deceive me, I have been spinning around you forever, how often must I send you my pleas for love. This is a poem addressed by a planet to the sun.)

I still know the poem by heart today. I still tremble when I read it. I did not know what the words meant but I knew instinctively, what they were trying to communicate.

And then slowly, on little thieves' feet, the horror stories of Jadugar Tengu and Himgauri along with Chandrakant Kakodkar, Dhananjay, Ajgar and the Tales of the Green Handkerchief…

'And then her cheeks grew warm….'

Or

'Then she blushed. And he…'

That kind of thing.

~

As the first petals began to unfurl, I did not find myself really interested in boys in that sense but there was a boy whom I did like very much in my class. He was older than me and always had a smile on his face. But his eye was on a girl called Kusum, who was also in our class.

Our teacher was an occasional visitor. This was Class III in a municipal school and Master Sahib did not feel there was much reason to teach anyone anything. When the teacher was away the boys would take the opportunity to tease the girls. The object of my affections would go and sit next to the object of his affections. She would simper shyly. Once he went so far as to touch her cheek. She went red. I got very angry. Here I was, hoping he would sit next to me, talk to me, tease me, and there he was, making up to that shrinking violet.

But that's as far as it went.

I never felt anything for any of the other boys. They also knew that I was different in some way. Whether we were eating lunch or playing or just getting on with it, the boys kept their distance. They were scared of me.

And so I read more and more as I grew and grew. My eyes were filled with dreams. My naiveté must have been there for all to read on my face. I was a thin girl with two plaits or sometimes a ponytail, a quiet girl, silent most of the time.

After my tonsillectomy, I suddenly shot up. I remained as thin as ever. My face changed a little, my hair was my inheritance from my mother. She lavished oil upon it, so much that it would drip down my face and I would look even more hesitant and harmless and pitiable than I would have otherwise. But my hair was black and thick and long for all that. When Bhai was in Mumbai, I would be taken everywhere: to meetings, sabhas, films, plays and exhibitions.

Bhai was fast friends with Atre Kaka.[17] Bhai would take me to his home on any number of occasions. His magnificent body and voice, his free and easy behaviour left me impressed and intrigued. He would also praise me. He would lend me books from his library, which seemed as big and sprawling as he was.

I did not see much of his wife[18] but I heard a lot about

---

[17]Acharya Atre or Prahlad Keshav Atre (1898-1969) was a prominent Marathi writer, poet, playwright and founder-editor of the newspaper *Maratha*.

[18]This probably refers to his second wife, Godavari Munge. This was an inter-caste marriage, too, and occasioned much comment. It was also rumoured that Atre had an affair with Vanamala, the actress in *Shyamchi Aai* and this caused his wife much grief.

her. She was erratic in her behaviour and was known to be rude. She did not like Bhai visiting. But even though I knew all this, I was curious about her.

She lived in such a big house, a bungalow really. She was so rich and yet her face revealed a deep discontent. How could she be so sad?

One day, we went over as usual. It was my birthday that day. She came out to talk to us.

'How thin you are, child,' she said. 'But you have a good head of hair. All your strength has gone into your hair, it seems. Is that a new frock? Is it your birthday? Oh my. Wait a moment.'

She went inside and brought us some sweets to eat. And she gave me a hair clip with a red stone in the shape of a flower.

I was delighted. And for a moment, I saw a different expression on that tormented and lined face, a secret expression, a fleeting one. Had she seen her own childhood reflected in my eyes?

~

Around this time, I was reading Vikram and Betaal stories, *Chandoba*, a magazine for children, as well as detective stories and *Zhep* (Reach) and *Zhunj* (The Fight) as well as the stories of Sarat Chandra Chatterjee, Marathi novels and short stories. And now a loneliness began to creep into my mind, uninvited, and sadness came with it.

What was sorrow? How did one feel as one endured it? I began to be drawn towards pain. I began to look forward to confronting its wounded Ashwatthama-esque face.[19] I was eager to be wounded in the same manner.

I was alone. I was sad. Or so I decided. What was happening? Why was I identifying myself with those melancholic heroines of the novels I was reading? Was it just an anguish for no reason? Or was this an augury of my life to come?

---

[19]Ashwatthama, a character in the *Mahabharata*, was cursed to have a bleeding sore on his face, from where a precious jewel was removed, after he tried to kill the Pandavas by night.

3

When I went to the fifth standard, I was enrolled at the Chhabildas Girls School at Dadar.[20] Didi had also studied at this school. This was where I began to come into my own, as my talents were given scope and I was encouraged to come out of my shell. I was at the top of my class—or near the top—in every subject except Mathematics. My English was also a bit raw but I got by on my achievements in other spheres and subjects. I was

[20]Chhabildas School at Dadar was one of the most important locations in the history of the development of experimental theatre in Mumbai. For more details see Shanta Gokhale's *The Scenes We Made: An Oral History of Experimental Theatre in Mumbai* (Speaking Tiger, 2015).

still excellent at bunking and at falling ill. In the sixth standard, some students were asked to take part in the school play. Harish Pitale[21] was choreographing a dance ballet. He cast me as a dancer. We were all treated as if we were his daughters. Chhabildas was also where I met Sulabha Deshpande, a well-known and brilliant theatre actor. She took us for an hour in Sanskrit and Hindi and directed the school play too.

Around October and November every year, there were interschool competitions in acting, singing, essays and elocutions. I would participate in everything. These were my debut performances. I used to dance well. My abhinaya and mudras were also good. My name began to be sent up every year for plays and for singing competitions. And I would always get the first prize.

I was good at Marathi. I loved Hindi, Sanskrit, Science and History. All the teachers were fond of me. The girls began to point me out to each other.

At home, too, my talents were encouraged. When guests came over, I was always asked to enact a scene from a play.

Things were going well. Bhai had bought sixteen-and-a-half acres of land at Boghegaon for a poetry village. We went to see it. Bhai had several plans afoot but the

[21]Harish Pitale was a renowned Bharatanatyam teacher. He was also guru to Jhelum Paranjape's mother. Jhelum Paranjape is an Odissi exponent of renown.

shacks were already built. The air was clean and breezes flowed freely; the sky above was clear and the weather was cool and pleasant. When a well was dug, they said, a living stream of water had gushed forth.

'So are all the other streams dead?' I asked.

Bhai told the contractor, 'Look, Lalaji, how well things are coming along. I tell you I have never done anyone any harm and so no one wishes me ill.'

Once Bhai, Aai and I went on a tour. We went to Hyderabad, Paithan, Alandi, Wambori, Nagar, Jalgaon, Aurangabad. I think this is where I got my taste for travel. I decided then that I wanted to see all that was beautiful in the world. I wanted to meet different people and see new places. I wanted to see every temple although I do not believe that one finds peace of mind there.

~

V. V. Bhatt—whom we called Dada—was the manager of Kalapathak. He looked after the correspondence. He was one of Bhai's closest friends. You could say that his daughter Rohini and I had been brought up together. Our friendship was the stuff of legend. I spent eight days of the month at their place. Both of us had identical frocks stitched for us. I loved the strict Brahminical regimen of their home. You got up early, did your surya namaskars, went for a walk. There was ghee in the buttermilk and bread to go with it. The food too was sweet. And all day we laughed: ha ha, khee, khee. Both our mothers disapproved of us laughing so much.

'What's there to laugh about?' they would ask.

Our nights were spent chatting and giggling. And we felt our bond to be so strong that it would last a lifetime.

~

1969. I was twelve years old.

Bhai was going to a programme in Indapur. Didi was going with him. Whenever he left, he would bid farewell to everyone. First Aai and this time, when he was standing on the staircase, he drew me close to him, and said, 'Why do you keep your distance from me, love?'

He kissed me and set me down and left.

Friday. Morning came. Only Aai and I were at home. At around 9 a.m., Dr Anand, one of Bhai's friends, came home. He was not his usual smiling self. His face was solemn, flushed. He told us that Bhai had been involved in an accident. For a moment, Aai was too stunned to respond.

She could only look at him. I did not understand anything. This had happened once before. After a very successful programme during his Goa election tour, the opposition was scared. They had stoned the car in which he was travelling. But his driver, Dattoo, had managed—with the help of police protection—to take the car into the jungle and escape. The opponents tried another tack.

They got hold of a doctor and forced him to announce Amar Shaikh's death in Goa after a brief illness. Everyone rushed to Goa in a panic. Acharya Atre sent his car. But they soon found out that it was a rumour.

Now Dr Anand entered our home with a telegram in his hand. He was serious. His wife was weeping. Aai was a stone statute. I still did not know what was going on. I could see that my mother's face was different: her lips were tight, her eyes empty of all feeling.

The accident had taken on the Indapur road at 2 a.m. A new driver was at the wheel. The vehicle was racing along through the night and in the darkness, the driver had thought there was a turn where there was none. When he realized his mistake, he stamped down on the brakes. Bhai shouted, 'Arré, arré, what are you doing?'

Before anyone knew what was going on, the Matador with its fifteen passengers turned turtle and rolled over three times. The top was sliced off. Everyone was screaming and shouting for help. But who was likely to come to their aid on that deserted stretch of road? Didi was sleeping with her head on Bhai's lap. She fell off her seat and landed on the floor of the van, escaping with only a few scrapes and bruises. But Bhai was thrown right out of the vehicle. A blood vessel near his brain was ripped open. There was blood everywhere. He was moaning in pain. The others were lying around. The petrol tank burst and the petrol fell on Mama. Kesarbai's long beautiful nose was broken in several places. In that state, trying to stanch the flow of blood from her nose, she went looking for the living. Didi came to her senses. A truck stopped to help. Until the police and help arrived, Didi sat by the side of her father's body, listening to his last tortured breaths.

Everyone was taken to the Sassoon Hospital in Pune. Bhai's body was brought to Mumbai by truck. Mama's body was in no state to be taken anywhere. He was cremated there.

The news spread like wildfire. The neighbourhood was filled with people and their noise. Our neighbours were weeping. The Communist Party, our friends and their families all came over. One of the neighbours was so shocked by the news that he had a heart attack and died.

Aai was silent through all this. She said not a word. She shed no tears. Bhai's body was laid out in the hall. I watched. I was quiet too. It was not as if I did not understand what was happening. But there were too many things happening to deal with, all in a huge lump.

Finally, his body was taken out and put into a truck.

'He really is going,' I thought and this unlikely thing started me crying, wailing, howling. That his last hug, that last cool touch…

After that I tried as best I could to wipe out the memory of him. I was frightened of the pain of being human. I wanted to forget. I was trying to escape. That was not very wise of me. I could avoid thinking about him but I could not erase the memories of him. They were in my bloodstream where they lay quietly, running deep in my veins, until suddenly, in unguarded moments, they would explode in my brain.

A man was leaving my life and I was watching helplessly. Others would also leave and I would be unable to do anything.

4

When Bhai died, the house was in good shape. Only the loan on the car had to be repaid. Our home had all the mod cons: a fridge, a phone. Within fifteen days of his passing, a friend got Didi a job in his bank. But the spirit of the house had been extinguished. It was empty, desolate, with only the thin voices of women echoing in it, women who nibbled at their food.

At the Coroner's Court, Didi was asked our religion.

'Humanism,' she said.

'We cannot write that. This is not our way,' they said, among other things. Didi was adamant. Finally, she got them to write 'Humanist' in the space for religion. That was a first in the history of the court.

The newspapers were full of Bhai. They carried stories about him, along with his picture. People wrote down their memories of him. They came and they went.

I remember Bhai was extraordinarily sensitive by nature. After a friend committed suicide, he was very upset. He was depressed for days and wandered about dejected.

When Anna Bhau Sathe[22] was ill, he brought him home. But before that we had gone to his place in the slum in Chirag Nagar, Ghatkopar. Our feet sank into the mud. His small hut was made of tin and asbestos sheets but he kept it very clean. There was little other than a clay water-pot and a small bust of Maxim Gorky in his room. We had to duck our heads to enter.

Bhai, V. V. Bhatt and I sat down on a mat and inhaled beedi smoke. Sathe was dark, with a high forehead and brown, cloudy eyes, somewhat mischievous and somewhat sad. Looking carefully at other people's faces was a childhood habit with me.

It was arranged that he should be taken to hospital and given special treatment. When Bhai went to see him, someone else was in the special room. Puzzled, Bhai came out and then he found Bhau on the floor, lying on a mattress.

Angrily, he went to inquire what had happened. The doctor pointed at the room.

---

[22]Anna Bhau Sathe (1920-1969) was a Dalit writer, folk poet and activist. He was a Communist for a while but began to follow Dr Babasaheb Ambedkar later.

'There he is. We gave him the room as requested.'

'Don't be silly,' said Bhai. He pointed to the man on the floor. 'That is Anna Bhau Sathe.'

'Him? So black?' The doctor asked and then shut his mouth and moved Bhau into the room.

When Bhau came home, I ran to him and caught hold of his hand and led him in.

'You've brought up the girl well,' he said to Bhai.

Bhai and Bharaskar got together and found him a room in Goregaon.

When Anna Bhau died, Bhai's face was dark and swollen with weeping. The actor Balraj Sahni offered a fitting tribute when he said: 'In the entire film industry, this was one man with a genuine social commitment.'

For three or four months, Anna Bhau's ashes lived with us, in a copper kalash. Someone said: 'Bhai, immerse those ashes soon. It's not a good idea to have them in the house so long.'

Bhai ignored him. From my childhood days, I knew that God was just a concept. There were no rituals, no rites, no religious programmes. That Bhai had been born a Muslim occurred to me only much later.

When anyone asked my caste in school, I would say, 'Human' with a fine disgust.

~

Bhai celebrated his fifty-first birthday in high style.

Khedkar the sculptor[23] and Sathe the painter and Rajdutt Kaka[24] all came over. It was an atmosphere rich with art and culture and how I luxuriated in it.

With Bhai's departure came the days of darkness. Our lives were now like a stage when the performance is over, a deserted theatre when the viewers have departed.

People stopped coming over. Didi would get up early, fill the water, cook and rush to work, while doing her MA at the same time. She was also in Yogen Desai's[25] dance group and went to Parvati Kumar's[26] dance classes. She

---

[23]B. R. Khedkar, noted realist sculptor, who has completed more than 375 bronze statues. He worked on the sets of *Mughal-e Azam* and is said to have created a rubber mask so that the male dancer Laxmi Narayan could look like Madhubala and perform some of the more intricate steps for her. (https://www.facebook.com/sculptorbrkhedkar/info)

[24]Rajdutt Kaka may refer to Datta Mayalu, one of the Marathi filmmakers of renown.

[25]Yogen Desai is said to have choreographed several dance ballets. Projesh Banerji in his book *Indian Ballet Dancing* (Abhinav Publications, 1983) says that they were of 'mostly on themes of interest and concern to people of Gujarat. These include *Ras Dulari* and *Chauladevi*.' He had his studio at Kala Bhavan, next to Opera House, and Asha Parekh was a leading lady and practised there.

[26]Acharya Parvati Kumar (1918-2012) trained in Bharatanatyam, Kathak and Kathakali but he was best known as a Bharatanatyam teacher. He established the Tanjavur Nritya Shala in Mumbai in 1968.

came home exhausted. But we didn't need much. How much do three women need? We had nearly overcome the shock of Bhai's death. My mother, though, was still very disturbed. She went to no functions. She gave up wearing saris with zari. But she did not give up her mangalsutra or her kumkum. The Communist Party had some influence on her. I liked saying how fair she was, how pink…and I also enjoyed how annoyed she got at this. Those dark eyes in her round face and on those cheeks, those dimples. Both of us would say, with pretend annoyance, 'Aai gave us nothing. She kept her fair skin for herself and she didn't even give us her dimples.'

She would snort and we would giggle.

Through all this I was writing poetry. Didi encouraged me. But we were still far away from the real relationship we would later share. I was somewhat in awe of her and there was that difference in our ages.

She was now acting in Rangayan's plays.[27] She had lots of friends: Bhakti [Barve], Sushama [Deshpande], Nima, Dilip Kolhatkar, Bal Karve among others. Didi's

---

[27]Rangayan was started as an experimental theatre group by actor-director Vijaya Mehta, playwright Vijay Tendulkar, and actors Shreeram Lagoo and Arvind Deshpande. It had a limited number of shows for each production as it conceived of each play as an experiment and once the experiment was conducted and replicated, the group should move on.

acting and dancing were extraordinary. She would give her all to her dancing. She was graceful, passionate and intensely involved in everything she did. Once I asked her, 'You're studying so much, struggling so much. What do you plan to do with it all?'

'I don't know,' she said.

Odd, I thought.

I, too, was acting in school plays. And during this time, I won the first prize in a poetry competition organized by Kalayatan, an organization based in Nasik. With the prize came a rotating trophy and the rather pompous title of Maharashtra Balkaviyatri (Child Poetess of Maharashtra), 1971-'72. That was the first of many prizes and much praise.

Once I took part in a singing competition. When I got there, I found that one was expected to sing to the accompaniment of the tabla and harmonium. This was a first for me. I got nervous. I was not sure I would be able to keep time with the tabla. Besides, the song I had chosen was a difficult one with many alaaps and fast taans: 'Jeevlaga rahile re, door ghar mazhe' (My love, I have wandered far away from home.) I sang it anyway and acknowledged the applause that followed. From the first alaap, it had seemed that everyone liked my singing. But I was unhappy. 'I don't think I sang well,' I mumbled and left the hall with a small face and went straight home.

The next day, the teacher gave me a silver medal. I had won the first prize.

~

One day, I found that my body was beginning to change. But I knew what was going on. I had always been a voracious reader and by the age of thirteen or fourteen, I had acquired a great deal of knowledge. I was curious about what went on between a man and a woman. I knew all about the physical changes that happen, how they happen and what menstruation meant and what I would have to do. I was waiting impatiently for it to happen.

And so the day arrived. I told Didi what had happened. Didi showed me what I must do, told me what was going on in my body. I pretended ignorance and put on an innocent expression as if I were hearing it all for the first time.

How odd I felt, how different inside. As if something were beginning, something slow and hesitant, a turning. My head was numb and there was a swirling in my blood. Aiyya, what was all this? Would my personality change because my body had changed? My own body was new to me. My eyes, my lips, over all of me a new set of sensations. And the bit below my waist seemed fatigued. It was all new and I was excited…

5

And then Aai began to behave strangely. She would take hold of a book and scribble away furiously. She would babble meaninglessly. She had been in the habit of writing earlier but she didn't have a style of her own now. Just words. Now she began to write incoherently. She would recite poems loudly whether she was in the bus or at home. She would move her eyes in a weird way. I didn't know what was going on. When Didi found out, she packed me off to Chembur to the home of a relative and began to investigate.

It was a nervous breakdown. Bhai's sudden death was making itself felt. Bhakti Barve was one of Didi's close friends. When Didi did not get leave, she would take Aai for shock treatment.

In a short while, Aai recovered. She might have been a graduate but she was not smart in the ways of the world. She did not get any benefits from what Bhai had achieved. Her mind was volatile; she could be distracted easily and confused just as easily. Didi and Aai did not get on anyway. Didi was annoyed out of all proportion by Aai's untidiness. She was fanatical about neatness. She kept herself in perfect condition. She often had words with me about my laziness. But I didn't bother too much. Aai couldn't cook so Didi had to get up in the morning and cook before going to work.

I did not miss a single school trip.

Didi did not let me feel any shortfall. Then came the all-important SSC year. I had dropped Mathematics so everyone expected me to do well. I had put my name down for singing classes but they did not hold my attention. Even though I had a good voice, I paid no heed to the class.

I began to study really seriously. I loved drawing on the floor. I learned this art from Aai. I sat for two art examinations. Now I began to draw diagrams of the heart and the eye on the floor.

I topped the preliminary examinations. I was also given the title of Best Student for all that I had achieved during the year. I had written the school play, directed it and acted in it as well.

~

One day, Mokashi Kaka[28] came over with some of his friends. Among them was Jayant Pradhan and Anil Barve.[29] They had come to solicit subscriptions for a journal they ran, called *Ranangan*. They were journalists and writers. And they had been stamped with the romantic title of Naxalites. Once they got to know us, they began to write letters. They came over once or twice. We became good friends and Didi freely admitted that she was considering Anil Barve seriously. Aai and I were delighted. I began to tease her. When Anil came over, I said, 'So you came for a yearly subscription and got yourself a life membership?'

Anil-bhaiyya became a regular at home. He was a loquacious and voluble sort, a happy person. The house began to come alive again. His friends would also stop by. Things were different now that there were men coming and going.

---

[28]This refers to Shyam Mokashi, the father of Paresh Mokashi, director of *Harishchandrachi Factory* (2009).

[29]Anil Barve is best known for his classic play *Hamidabaichi Kothi* (Hamida's Kothi).

Eating and talking were Anil-bhaiyya's greatest hobbies. We chatted a great deal.

Didi and Anil-bhaiyya agreed on an early marriage. The Barve family opposed the match. When Didi went to meet them, someone said, 'You'll have to change your religion.'

Didi replied, 'When I have no belief in religion, where's the question of changing it?'

Finally, Anil-bhaiyya came to Saat Rasta to stay with us. The marriage was a big occasion. Theirs was a registered marriage with a reception in the evening. I enjoyed dressing up very much and so I went all out for the wedding. I could feel the appreciative eyes of the male guests on me. I discovered that there are many different ways to appreciate a person.

~

A poet of great sensibility was in the habit of praising my poems lavishly. His appreciation took the form of looking at me with love in his eyes but he could not bring himself to say anything. I had no idea that I was toying with him for he only made me laugh. Such letters he would write: page after page of poetic prose. I would show those to letters to Didi and we would giggle over them.

I began to write him letters too. They were juicy letters, adorned with quotations, decorated with polysyllabic words. But that had been my nature from the very beginning, the role I had chosen for myself: she who lived her life without counting the cost, she who threw herself at experiences, all that kind of thing.

He would come over, intense but confused, and I felt sorry for him. I felt that I shouldn't be doing this. But I gave him no sign, no hint of whether I liked him or not.

I had already an image of my Prince Charming in my head. He would be a maverick, a poet, good-looking, dark, a macho man with male energy to spare.

My poor poet had none of these requirements. As I grew into womanhood, I began to act what I imagined to be the role: I would look into mirrors and simper, I would behave coy. I began to like the look of saris, specially those draped over my nubile body. I had dreams in my eyes and in those dreams I planned everything: the appropriate lines from the films I had seen, the beauty aids that would go with my saris and make-up, the bungalow I would have and where the piano would be placed; the French windows through which the light would flood; the way the air would flow, free and unimpeded and happy through my home and its vast library; the ornamental pond with its decorative fish, red and gold flickers in the water; the bakul tree I could see through the window, the gulmohur and the raat ki rani. Beyond these the dense jungle and a footpath of red earth running into it.

They say that even a donkey can look beautiful when the bloom of youth is upon her. Something like that happened with me as well. I did not, however, see myself as beautiful. I thought of myself as smart; the girl with the brains. I had read no ideology. But there was a change in my poetry.

Once the poet Atmaram Patil read my poems. He praised them and then he added, 'You're still self-centred. You have to get out of this. Look at the world around you. Or your poetry will not improve. These are self-absorbed.'

I thought about what he said. And I read the poems again.

To think, to dream, to scan the self, these were my obsessions. Each poem, I hoped, showed a different mood. But now I began to see another set of ideas creep into my poems. I had begun to develop a social consciousness. Without willing it, I was responding to my social context, expressing my hatred of injustice and inequality. This continues even today. I was not forcing it. I was not posing. This was not a matter of style. I have not been able to change this.

I was not in the habit of reading the newspapers. The current debates, the issues of the day, the social questions, Marxism, all these were words I had heard but had not paid attention to. So where had these concerns come from? I did not have to make much of an effort. The poems just flowed. In minutes they would be complete.

Without my changing a word, they would settle into place. And then a full-stop, following which contentment, one that I have experienced again and again, after writing a poem, after finishing a painting. When I had made my entry in a play, when I had danced alone and with abandon as I listened to a song on the radio, when I had watched a good film. There was no limit to the joy I felt in my creation. But equally the creations of other artists could fill me with joy. This continues even today.

6

Didi had good news for us: she was expecting. Her pregnancy seemed full of fun and laughter. People began to visit again. *Ranangan* was proceeding apace. Anil-bhaiyya was a man of tremendous energy. He was full of jokes. His conversation was witty and subtle.

And then came February 1974.

To get hot scoops for *Ranangan*, Anil-bhaiyya had to get around. And so he landed up at a meeting of a new political organization called the Dalit Panthers at Worli on February 6. The elections were fast approaching. These new young Dalit leaders were hot-heads, their ideas inflammatory. A new energy was moving among them. At base, the Dalit Panther movement was the brainchild of the fantastic Namdeo Dhasal.

He was a friend of Anil-bhaiyya. He would wear a necklace of big pearls and wander everywhere. He looked like a goat about to be offered to the gods or a bullock that had been decorated for Pola.[30] His trousers were of many colours, patched together from various pieces of cloth, as a quilt might be.

At this time, a violent angry terrorist organization called the Black Panthers had been started in America. This was a movement to take by force the civil rights that White America had denied them. This was the basic idea on which Namdeo Dhasal based his Dalit Panthers. J. V. Pawar[31] also helped. People were gathered by beating on thalis. In the next six months, a group of angry young men like Raja Dhale[32] came together. Some sympathetic Socialist leaders also offered them support.

In general, the Left made much of the Dalit Panthers. Perhaps they hoped to take these useful young men

---

[30]Pola is a festival in which bulls are decorated and worshipped on the new-moon day in the month of Shravan (around August). It commemorates the killing of Polasur by Krishna when He was a child.

[31]J. V. Pawar is a noted author and poet. He was a founder member of the Dalit Panthers and editor of *Vidrohi* and *Dhammalipi*.

[32]Raja Dhale was one of the founder members of the Dalit Panthers, according to his Wikipedia entry, and then joined the Republican Party of India where he led the Raja Dhale faction. He contested elections for Parliament from the Bharipa Bahujan Mahasangh.

under their wing. That was it. The Dalit Panthers became a political party. The newspapers wanted to destroy it and so they praised it to the skies.

They called their first public meeting around the elections. And of course, there was trouble at the meeting. The police were out in full force. Cases were filed against the party for the obscene and abusive speeches that were made—these were the abuses that they piled upon the ruling classes, their perverted behaviour and decadent ways.

A warrant was put out for Namdeo Dhasal. As usual, he had slipped away after making his speech. He made contact with Anil-bhaiyya. They came home with two or three other men.

Namdeo was extraordinarily good-looking compared to the men around him, a rough sort, tall, thin but with a strong body. He was dark but his features were chiselled, cruel, arrogant. As opposed to this, a pair of laughing eyes that seemed capable of love. His laugh rang out free, joyous, without guile. His behaviour showed self-confidence, arrogance, the commanding presence of a general.

I only saw him that day. We were not introduced. Anil-bhaiyya was in a hurry to file on this hot issue and they were both immersed in the interview. The interview was in full swing. He came over again a few days later. He didn't say much and that made me angry.

Who did he think he was? Other young men fell all over themselves to talk to me, and this one? I knew he was a poet. I had read *Golpitha*. I hadn't understood much of it but in the poems that I had understood, what came across clearly was his power. There was something enigmatic and terrible and magnetic all at once. The poems drew you in. It was as if some carnivorous animal was lurking inside them and its claws would reach out and score your body...

~

A poetry reading is in progress. The organizer receives a note that someone in the audience would like to read a poem.

Anant Kanekar[33] is in the chair. The stage is filled with a bunch of respectable and well-known poets. And in the middle of this a taxi-driver wants to read his poems? Such speaking shrugs. The taxi driver climbs quietly on to the stage and begins to read. The audience is stunned. Something odd and huge is happening. The content of these poems, their raw power, is completely different from all the other poems being read on stage. This is recognized immediately and he is given permission to read another one. But he has won this round and he

[33]Anant Kanekar (1905-1980) was a lawyer, poet and writer. He edited magazines like *Chitra* and *Asha*. He taught at Khalsa College and Siddharth College, both in Mumbai.

allows this wave of victory to sweep him out of the hall. He vanishes. That is Namdeo Dhasal.

He lives in a slum at the foot of Usha Kiran.[34] He smokes ganja all day and sleeps in a taxi all night. He lives in the eye of the storm and seems to be drawn to the Socialists. That was where he began to write poetry. He comes from the infamous red-light area and is used to living with several vices, all of which he vomits out in his poetry.

He fell in love young and eloped with the girl to Pune. The girl is of a higher caste and her family is powerful. They take her away from him. And in the heart-break of that, a good student is ruined.

His mother tried her best to hammer sense into him, but once a boy slips free, he is gone forever. He did one year of a fine-art course and then went off to the village and wandered about. He filled up on alcohol, charas, ganja, opium and Laal Pari[35] and learned to drive a taxi. He tried everything: the whores, the bodies that presented themselves. He distilled the life of Golpitha and poured it out, bringing it alive in his poetry.

---

[34]Usha Kiran is a multi-storey building on Mumbai's M.L. Dahanukar Marg (aka Carmichael Road). It was built in the mid-1960s and for many years was the only multi-storey building on the street.

[35]Indian alcohol is classified into IMFL (Indian Made Foreign Liquor) and Country. Laal Pari is a popular brand of country alcohol.

He was now wandering about with a manuscript: Golpitha. By the edge of the sea, he met Narayan Athavale.[36] Some of the poems had been printed in *Satyakatha*.[37] Athavale told him that he should get *Golpitha* printed. The hut in which the Dhasals lived was leaking; there was no money for tin sheets to cover it. And so he handed over the manuscript for two hundred rupees.

Golpitha created a storm in the world of Marathi letters. Its elegant outlines, its carefully manicured beauty was wiped out by one Namdeo Dhasal. His words were cruel, savage. They were words that could not be easily understood and yet they felt like an attack. It was difficult to believe in the world they conjured up; it was impossible not to believe in it. Who could write like that? It was as if someone savage had arrived in the secret garden of poetry and was going to uproot all the values we had nurtured.

~

[36]Narayan Athavale (1933-2011) was an editor, writer and later a Member of Parliament from the Shiv Sena. At the time that he published *Golpitha*, he was working with the *Loksatta*, the Marathi newspaper published by the Indian Express Group.

[37]*Satyakatha*, printed at Mouj Printing Press, was a little magazine, one of many that were launched in the 1970s in the Marathi sphere. It was started by S. P. Bhagwat, V. P. Bhagwat and Ram Patwardhan.

Namdeo was the only child of his parents. Other children had been born but they had died. And so he was the apple of their eyes. There are different ways of loving—Mahar love is one of them. When a boy does something wrong, you hug him. When your son runs away with a girl, you abet him in his elopement.

Namdeo's father worked in a mutton shop in the Fort. His job involved carrying entire carcasses of goats and carving them up. At that time, he would get forty rupees a day and some mutton, too. In those days, a man who earned forty rupees a day was doing quite all right. But since his parents had no control over their spending, it all went on food and drink. They had no habit of saving. His father gave Namdeo a rupee every day until he stopped working. Then he gave him even more.

His mother was very—one might say excessively—loving and innocent, too. She was a beautiful woman and remained lovely even in old age.

~

And so Namdeo began the Dalit Panthers. Wandering around the city through the night was part of the deal. He was always ready for a fight. Speeches, meetings, travelling, this was the life of the romantic revolutionary. But whenever he returned home, and he usually did so with any number of friends, his mother was always ready with a meal.

If the food were over, she'd cook more: kheema, mutton and bhakri.

Namdeo was riding a wave of popularity. He was a front-ranking Dalit leader and a poet. He was famous. He came to us trailing clouds of love: the love of his parents, the love of his friends and associates, the love of society.

After a couple of visits, he even began to talk to me. He had heard that I wrote poetry, too. The riots at Worli had begun.[38] He would turn up in the evening or in the middle of the night. Sometimes, there would be a couple of others with him. Then Anil and he would sit down and plan strategy. This was all about soda-water bottles, acid bulbs, violence. No one could get in to the chawl, no one could get out. The police had surrounded it. So now the discussion would turn to how to change tacks, where to start again. As a taxi-driver, Namdeo knew every corner and backstreet of the city as if there were maps in his mind. They would talk about how to make bombs. All this seemed revolutionary and romantic to me. They could talk until two or three in the morning. My job was to keep the tea coming.

Once when the riots had cooled down a bit, he came over alone. He began to talk to me. I was in a skirt and blouse, my hair in plaits. I was sitting in my usual style,

[38]The riots were between the Shiv Sena and the Dalit Panthers.

on a swing, with a bolster on my lap, one leg dangling. He said he'd read my poems in the papers and liked them. He asked if he could look at my poetry book. I let him take the notebook and, that very day, he was arrested. Thus it was that he got to read my poems in jail, with his comrades-in-arms. The notebook went with him from jail to jail—Chembur, Agripada, Bhoivada. He made the rounds of all the lock-ups and my notebook went with him and was read by everyone.

I gave up hope of ever retrieving it.

~

Anil-bhaiyya wrote scripts for the movies. His friend Gajanan Jahagirdar would direct films based on the stories he wrote.

Jahagirdar had a huge bungalow at Lonavla. And so it was agreed that Anil-bhaiyya should go there to write in the quietness of a hill-station. I was preparing for the examinations and it was decided that the change of air would do me good and the quiet would help me study and so we set out.

The clean clear air, the trees, the open sky, the huge airy bungalow were wonderful. The Jahagirdar couple was very sweet to me. I was excited but still trying to focus on my studies. But when I get close to nature I tend to lose it. The days passed in a wonderful haze of long walks, mischievous conversations with Anil-bhaiyya, chats with the Jahagirdars, great meals and a little studying now and again.

Then one night the bell rang. It was Anil-bhaiyya's friend, Jayant Pradhan. He too was a revolutionary; he had been a union leader in his time; he was a card-carrying Communist. With him, the poet Namdeo Dhasal.

His clothes were the colour of dirt, his hair matted. He had a jhola on his shoulder and a Chinar cigarette dangling from his lips. This style had become the model for all the young men in those days. The shabnam bag, the Chinar cigarette and the beard. There he was with the same free seductive laughter and the same dark strong-featured face.

We ate and all that sort of thing. He said that he liked my poetry very much. We began to chat. He told us tales of police harassment, police torture.

I expressed my sympathies.

'In a political movement, there is no room for the personal,' he said.

Anil-bhaiyya would joke, 'Hey Raju, what studying are you talking about? You've been on page 315 since yesterday.'

He had brought a camera along. I draped myself in a sari and coquetted as he took photographs of me. The wind was rain-wet.

'Do you like the rain?'

'Very much.'

'Me too.'

In that poetry-soaked atmosphere, two poets were drawing close. Jahagirdar had noticed this. So had Anil-bhaiyya. But I was not aware of any of this. I did not know anything about his earlier life or family. I only knew his poetry. I knew he was a poet, a sensitive and (very!) Left-leaning poet. And he fit in with my ideal: masculine, maverick, sensitive, a poet to love and to love me.

That night, Anil-bhaiyya asked me, 'Do you like him? What do you think?'

Shameless, I said: 'I do like him.'

'I liked the idea of the two of you together,' he said. 'He's a poet. You are, too. Should I talk to him?'

'Not right now.'

That day, he was called to give an account of himself. This upset him a little. He left the room annoyed. I called him into another room and closed the door.

'What do you feel for me?' I asked, staring at him.

He was silent for a few moments. Then he raised his gaze to mine. My hair began to stand on end, my heart to pound. His eyes were laughing. He looked at me and asked, 'Must I say it?'

My eyes dropped shyly and I blushed.

The next day he left. At the time of departure, he smiled.

'I'm off.'

'Yes.'

He offered his hand.

I was thrown into confusion but I put my hand in his. An electric current ran through my body. He held my hand for a moment, pressed it, let it go. He raised his hand in a salute.

'Laal salaam,' he said.

I laughed aloud and he pulled his beret down over his eyes, laughed and walked away, looking back from time to time.

On the day before he left, he had taped me singing. Until the next time we met, he would play this tape again and again, make his friends listen to it, right up to two in the night, praising me all the while. His friends must have listened, sleepy and irritated, for they were forced to chime in with praise for my singing. Inside, they must have been laughing at him.

~

When we returned from Lonavla, Anil-bhaiyya announced to Aai: 'Your second daughter is getting married.'

Aai was stunned.

'Isn't she a bit too young to be making these decisions?'

Didi found out about this when she got back from the office. Things were strained at home. Anil-bhaiyya and Didi had a series of intense high-level discussions.

Didi was against the match. She thought I was too

young and my education was incomplete. I had no business thinking about love and marriage. But she had no specific objections to Namdeo as such.

And so a dozen different winds of opinion began to blow through the house. I was caught in the middle and suddenly I broke out in chicken-pox. The pustules appeared all over my body and a fever wracked my frame. I was thrashing about like a fish out of water.

The examinations were approaching. I could not even bear the touch of cloth on my body. Didi spent the night applying neem leaves all over my body.

In a while, the fever broke but the pustules remained. Jahagirdar might have invited me to stay at his place but when he came to see me, he did not come into the room. Anil-bhaiyya invited him in but he said, 'No, she won't like it.'

I found this remarkable. How much understanding of human nature he had displayed. He was a natural director. Which young woman would like her disfigured face to be seen?

I was pale and gaunt. The next day Namdeo came, bearing a huge bouquet of bright red roses. I did not like him coming and told Anil-bhaiyya so. Namdeo said to him gently, 'Arré, everyone looks beautiful to the eyes of love,' and he came in, gave me the flowers, talked a while and left.

I had not even studied much because of all this.

Chicken-pox is contagious so I might not even have been allowed to sit for the examinations. But Mr and Mrs Bhatt persuaded the teachers to allow me to appear and I was given a separate bench. I would go to the examination hall with a fever. I had not even bathed properly in days. I just managed to write somehow. I didn't even know what I was writing. I was sure I would fail.

After the exams, I was free. I had warned Namdeo off for the period of the examinations. He turned up on the very next day. I loved the colour white. I loved white saris. He came with five or six gajras. And although my family was not too keen on the match, we were still given our privacy. So free was the atmosphere that we were even allowed to go out together.

Up to this point, he had not so much as touched me. But that day, he took my hand in his and kissed it.

I remember thinking that this was a rather poetic gesture.

He went off to Nagpur and returned with a sari for me and a huge painting by Bhau Samarth.[39] I was interested

---

[39]Bhau Samarth (?-1991), Nagpur-based painter, is mentioned in Omprakash Valmiki's autopbiography *Joothan*, translated by Joel Kuortti as 'a poet, a painter and a true human being.' He has a gold medal in painting named after him, conferred by the Nagpur University.

in painting but I did not much like abstraction nor did I understand it. Those dark brooding colours made no sense. Black and blue or red and black in combination hurt my eyes…

We began to go around together. Films, plays, gardens, the sea. We never used the train or the bus. Either we took taxis or we walked. And we walked a great deal. I got to see every inch of the city. Kamathipura, Pila House,[40] the brothels and the women standing in the windows, doors, streets…dark women, their short gaudily-coloured skirts showing their thighs, their tight low-necked blouses stretched as they stood, arms akimbo, making suggestive gestures to prospective clients, experienced young men, well-seasoned youth. I was shocked at all this. Namdeo knew all the hoodlums and toughs there. The writer J. V. Pawar also lived somewhere there in a chawl full of hijras who would hoist their saris and perch on the wall. These unholy and disgusting creatures frightened me; I felt like a timid rabbit confronted with all this. And yet the will to live seemed strong in this dehumanized world. What was it that made them want to go on?

Everywhere we went Namdeo introduced me as his wife.

~

[40]Pila House is in the Lamington Road-Grant Road area. It was once Play House for that is where many of the theatres were. Local usage made it Pila House.

One day, we left home in the morning and we roamed a great deal. There was always another friend to meet, another conversation to have, another cup of tea.

We ended up having a huge discussion with Sunil Dighe[41] on the Panthers. There were decisions to be made and course corrections to be effected. All this went on from 4 p.m. right up to ten in the night. I was bored. When I got home, the house was in an uproar. Everyone thought I had eloped. Didi was furious. She had much to say and she said it at length. I was silent. I was forbidden from going out with Namdeo. After that, he would sometimes try to suck up to Anil-bhaiyya. Or he would send a note with someone. It would be passed to me as I served tea and then I would read it and slip out to meet him.

One night we met at the sea. It was a dark night lit only by a handful of laughing stars and filled with the deep serious rumble of the sea. His arms were hard and strong around me, his breath hot as were his kisses. 'Someone might see,' I remember thinking. I felt shy and scared as well. I was trying to keep his stormy passion under control. Around us I could hear other couples. In the darkness, I could barely make out their silhouettes. I got up quickly.

---

[41]Sunil Dighe is now a lawyer. Then he taught at the Mumbai University and was a founder-member of the Dalit Panthers.

Many of Namdeo's Leftist friends and others were in favour of us marrying. Namdeo was now a politician. He was committed to Leftist ideology. The Dalit Panthers were growing in strength and were now a force to reckon with. Namdeo was a good organizer. He was seen as the man who could give the movement some direction.

Then Namdeo invited Aai, Didi, Anil-bhaiyya and me over to his home for a meal. I was going to see his home for the first time. It was in a single room. Right next to it were some small-scale factories and waste-paper shops. There was a lot of pollution. The next lane was filled with the brothels of Pila House and Foras Road. All of it was lit by a dirty yellow exhausted light. Faded quilts, piles of tins. In one corner, a huge brass bed, and so much stuff piled on to it, you could not see the mattress. Blackened tins, a clay oven, a few vessels, one or two boards on which some other things were kept, and near the door a lovely wooden cage in which a pair of lovebirds billed and cooed at each other.

None of this shocked me. I was in my own world but Aai and Didi were horrified. That such a cosseted child should come to a place like this to live seemed incredible to them. And then our cultural backgrounds were so different. What if he were a poet? And much more of the same.

His father was a little hard of hearing. He had just given up working but he was quite happy. But then his expectations from life were few and simple. My laughing and my babbling are two inseparable parts of my nature. I have an unstoppable stream inside me and a seven-storey laugh. Namdeo did not like these things. Not that he said so in the beginning.

~

After wandering around with Namdeo in Golpitha, I remembered something. During our SSC year, there was a tall, smart, somewhat mannered girl in our class. Many of the other girls had told me she was 'fast', that she roamed around with boys after school. There is always a bunch like that in every class. Since I was the class leader, I had to try and behave even-handedly with everyone. This girl was a fan of my singing and thought highly of my intelligence. She was open in her affection. She would ask after me, help me, try to get close to me.

She often invited me home. I'd say I would come and put her off but one day she simply bore me off with her. Her home was somewhere in Sandhurst Road, an area to which I had never been. She lived in a chawl. It was an untidy room with things scattered about. I was quite surprised to see a house like that. But then I said to myself: 'It's not just cleanliness and beauty that makes a house a home. So even in such a place true bonds may be formed.'

I went in. Her mother welcomed me. She seemed like

mothers everywhere: plump, her tousled hair twisted up into a knot, her sari hitched up to get on with the housework.

She was happy to see me.

'She tells me so much about you. I'm so happy you made it at last,' et cetera. First the kitchen and then the living room. When I went into that room, I got the shock of my young life. In the middle of all the clutter, there was a body lying twisted on the floor. It was a young man of about twenty or twenty-one but his face was different, contorted. His dull unseeing eyes wandered at random. Saliva dribbled from his mouth in a small stream. Flies covered him.

'My brother,' she said calmly. 'He had a stroke when he was a child. His brain didn't develop. It's remained the mind of a six-month-old. We have to do everything for him, from feeding him to cleaning him.'

My hair stood on end. This was the first time I had seen anything like it.

'I never feel like coming home. So after school, I wander about. Which girl will come with me after school? That's why I go with the boys.'

I wanted to forgive her a hundred times over for the sins ascribed to her.

'Sometimes I clean him up. Generally, Aai does it but after school, it's my turn…'

'Doctors?' I mumbled. 'Some treatment?'

'We've tried everything. Nothing worked.'

This was clear from looking at him. I felt guilty. I was nauseated. What things happen! What would happen to this boy? What would happen to his mother? How would she be able to look after a fully-grown young man with a six-month-old brain? How could she do this when she knew there was no hope of improvement? What a terrible life.

She now put some bhajyas onto a plate and put them in front of me. I found it difficult to get even words out. How was I going to get food in? I had no taste for it either. Her mother understood and took the plate into the kitchen so I could eat there, away from the sight, but none of that tasty food would go down. In the next room, the man-boy was babbling. He was twisting and writhing on the floor, like a crab whose legs and pincers have been broken.

Oh God!

I could not stop myself from asking: 'Why don't you put him on some bedding? At least a sheet?'

'He dirties them. He can't speak so he can't tell us when he wants to go. And he doesn't stay on the sheet if you put one under him. What can I give you?'

Finally, I managed to force some food down. I felt so guilty. I had a home of my own, a good home, people around me who would give me anything I wanted.

Later, that girl and I became good friends. I never revealed her secret to anyone but I never visited her home again, either.

That memory came back vividly as I wandered through Golpitha that day. In those chawls, behind those doors, those windows, were thousands of people like that man-boy, some deaf, some dumb, some challenged in other ways. I could see no difference in the lifeless eyes of that boy, turned towards a patch of sky, and the eyes of these women. Numbed with the curse of prostitution, their broken souls cast down from the earth, unable to take one living breath. What will erase all this? And when?

~

Namdeo began to push for an early wedding. When Didi told him that I could not marry until I finished my BA, he began to calculate how many days there were in four years. Then one day, he got annoyed.

'If you won't marry me now,' he threatened, 'I'll marry someone else.'

I got angry too. We began to argue. When I decided to break off with him, he appeared the next day and tried a different approach; this time he was all lovey-dovey and I melted. We fixed a date. He had been to prostitutes often in the past. And when he got the clap, he'd taken treatment as well. But he was still afraid to lay hands on me.

After the wedding date had been fixed, Didi went to Pune and Aai went to Boghegaon on some farm work. He told me, 'It's fun to do it before the wedding. Afterwards, it becomes a matter of routine.'

I said nothing. He kept talking. I tried to explain. I did not know much about what happened between a man and a woman. He became impatient. I was shy.

Didi's brother-in-law Shirish was at home. We were all there. Latif-bhaiyya (Namdeo's friend), Namdeo, me and Shirish. We went out for a film and a meal. That was the first time I tasted beer. I began to fly a little. We went home and were sitting together in the room when he asked:

'Giving?'

'What?'

'Your womanhood.'

And before I could answer, he had his hand over my mouth.

Baap ré, that first time was nothing but pain. I wondered how anyone could get any joy out of this circus. It hurt so much… But I liked surrendering my body to the man I loved. The whole thing was a bit awkward and I discovered that women are much more beautiful than men. Without their clothes on, there's something a bit repulsive about men.

Exhausted, we fell asleep. There was no pleasure that night for me, only pain.

~

We had set the date for May. The wedding shopping began. Namdeo bought everything from Pune: pots and pans and all the other things we needed to set up home. Fearing that I might die if he asked me to live in that terrible neighbourhood, he put down a deposit of two thousand rupees for a one-room, one-kitchen with a toilet and bathroom in Bandra. The area was a nice one, even if it was off the beaten track. The room was airy and cosily tucked away. It had been painted before we moved in. The wedding preparations finally ended. Because I did not want to worry about children so soon, Aai took me to a gynaecologist. The wedding date was fixed: 1 June, 1974. We didn't want to spend too much. Didi was still upset. And so we pruned the list of invitees down to the minimum. We decided also to get married at home. I made my preparations. Didi gave me some saris and jewellery.

1 June, 1974. I was dressed up. At that time, 'natural beauty' was still considered the best kind of beauty. Didi believed in this too. We didn't visit beauty parlours. I was delicate, thin, dark, underage but I went into the wedding, guarding my childish joy.

Since I was against the idea of having any religious rituals—either Buddhist or Vedic—the only option was to have a registered marriage. But I was too young for that.

People gathered, those closest to us, a select few. Some who were close but were not invited have still not forgiven us.

The night before my wedding Mrs V. V. Bhatt took me home with her. I had grown up in their house too and Mrs Bhatt had treated me as her daughter. Rohini was one of my closest friends. She and I laughed and cracked jokes all night. In the morning, Mrs Bhatt gave me a bath, and smeared me with turmeric and uthna.[42] I then came home. Not one of those who loved me were happy at me getting married but I could see nothing of this.

The guests gathered. Four o'clock came and went but there was no sign of the bridegroom. Someone said, 'Odd! No sign of the boy yet! Hey Raju, isn't he coming then, this husband of yours? You'd think he'd be on time for his own wedding at least!'

Finally Namdeo did show up. He put a garland around my neck. I put one around his. And then he decided to give a little speech.

'Now that we have chosen each other as life partners, we must look after each other with love and understanding. I accept her as my wife. Our bond is the

[42]Uthna is a home-made exfoliant (made of various herbs and spices) which is applied to the body before a bath.

social concern that we share and so we will direct our lives towards definite goals but still…' and much more of the same.

~

There! Married!

~

We left that night for Bandra. Uninvited, a whole lot of Namdeo's friends, poets, party functionaries and the like came over. The house was filled with people. As I changed my sari, I thought to myself: 'It's a good thing we finished our honeymoon before marriage. Or else my first night would have been spent in this crush of people.'

~

The next morning, demonstrating great consideration for us, the whole jingbang lot vamoosed. Our honeymoon began. I could now enjoy his companionship. A sexual relationship is a delicate and difficult question. Once the strings are tuned, the music is supposed to last a lifetime. If they're not, the discord begins to affect your harmony in other spheres as well. That may be because this physical relationship is the basis of all others. You keep looking for signs or clues to who he is but even so, you may never feel that you have understood him fully. Be that as it may, once flesh has recognized flesh, then an extraordinary and amazing feeling arises once the natural desires have been quenched, when the other person has become part of your mind and body and by his responses to you gives you an understanding of himself. They say there are thirty-six qualities[43] that should match between a husband and wife. But even if not one matches, you get on with it, especially after the children arrive. But the dialogue between the bodies is a must. For right up to this day, the male animal cannot go beyond a woman's body. And so the only link is forged in the realm of the physical.

I did not know how to cook at all. Namdeo taught me how to make chapattis. He would do things like cutting the onions and handing them over. Until then, I had not so much as picked up a cup and saucer for myself, but now I was learning enthusiastically. The chawl in which we were staying was clean and pleasant but all the women were domestic workers. It was a workers' basti and no one was willing to come so far to clean the house for me. I began to wash the dishes and the clothes, clean the house and sweep. Namdeo looked on appreciatively. The household goods were in place. The market was quite far away. I had no idea how to cook vegetables. I could manage the lentils—moong and masur dal, which I cooked alternately—but that was about it. But I kept the

---

[43]A rather complicated astrological calculation involving everything from birth signs to class positions.

house shipshape. Namdeo had many books on politics and literature. I began to read them. This was where I had my first lessons in Marxism. I started making notes. I would often ask him to explain something to me but that didn't work for him. He would say, 'Read the books.'

~

In all the hustle and bustle of the wedding, the Dalit Panther movement was eclipsed. But who began the arguments and how they assumed the proportions they did is still difficult to understand. The movement had drawn many people to it. Since Namdeo seemed to have Leftist leanings, both the Communist Party of India and the Communist Party (Marxist) helped a lot. They supported him with money for court fees and paid the lawyers' bills. Not a single party was working among the Dalits. So everyone wanted to bring this young party of hot-blooded youth into their fold.

I did not know much about politics but I had an intuitive understanding of human psychology and the nature of people. Raja Dhale was a bit egoistic but sober; Namdeo was innocent and foolish and open but a hooligan at heart. He had no pragmatism in him. He used language which at that time was thought to be obscene and was more than what most people could stomach; he abused with the greatest of ease. He was rough, a maverick, arrogant, uncaring and often resorted to violence. He could often be autocratic but he also had a golden tongue. He was a good orator and he was quick to forge alliances and as quick at breaking them. He also had a sensitive and thoughtful side. He was slow to anger but in a rage, he was terrifying. He was difficult to be with; he was the sultan of whimsy. He planned nothing. There was no discipline in the party. The rules were on paper only. Problems about money began. Just before the morcha protesting the martyrdom of Bhagwat Jadhav,[44] Namdeo accused Raja Dhale and J. V. Pawar of taking money from the Congress. The Panthers had stayed away from electioneering; they had not aligned themselves to any party but after this, the whole picture of the election changed. Rosa Deshpande[45] was elected and the Dalit Panthers suddenly acquired political significance. Namdeo's *Jahirnama* (Manifesto) played an important role in that. Namdeo's position was consistent, offering inspiration to the Dalit movement. He defined Dalit in a very inclusive manner and that gave the movement a solid ideological base. The newspapers made him into a household name. There were interviews, articles, columns written about him. A romantic aura began to gather around the Dalit Panthers. All the progressives,

---

[44]Bhagwat Jadhav was killed in January 1974 during a morcha when a grinding stone was hurled at the crowd.

[45]Union leader and organizer Rosa Deshpande was S. A. Dange's daughter. She was named for Rosa Luxemburg (1871–1919), Marxist theorist and philosopher.

the Leftist parties, the Right-wing ones, everyone including the Republican Party of India began to look at these young men with hope. The suffering of Namdeo Dhasal had a name now: Dalit Panther. People started wondering about them and from across the world, revolutionaries, journalists, poets and even lawyers came to meet him, to interview him or to discuss politics with him. Namdeo was always wary; he felt that some of them had come to try and buy him and so he kept them at arm's length.

He was specially careful of the Americans and their various emissaries; he gave them short shrift. He did not feel as much dislike for Brahmins as he felt for these people. In the early days, when the Shankaracharya was giving a discourse in Pune and had begun to talk about the chaturvarna system and its importance, Namdeo had thrown a shoe at him. The Shankaracharya had collapsed and everyone around began to scream and shout in shock. The five-thousand strong audience was furious. An old man sitting next to Namdeo lassoed him with his shoulder-cloth and tried to take him to the police. How Namdeo managed to get out with the help of his boys is another romantic story.

When it had been decided that no interviews would be granted, Namdeo talked to the capitalist-owned weekly *Manohar*[46] and offended all the others. The work of the

[46] A mainstream magazine published by the Kirloskars.

organization began to be ignored and personal issues were foregrounded. There were many who simply added fuel to the fire but those we always have with us.

Fame acquired quickly is neither very real nor is it very long-lasting. It was my opinion that the newspapers had conspired to wreck the movement and those with entrenched interests had provided the fuel. There are two ways to hurt someone politically: one is to ignore them totally and the other is to praise them disproportionately. And finally the split became clear. One group coalesced around Raja Dhale, the other stayed with Namdeo Dhasal. Finally, both suffered because of the rift and it had its impact everywhere. Raja and his group spread it abroad that Namdeo was a Communist and he was teaching the Dalit Movement lessons in Communism and so destroying it. Many rumours and anecdotes, all spread by Raja Dhale and his followers, were rife.

'The watch he wears? Dange gave it to him which is why he takes such good care of it!'

'He married the Communist daughter of a Communist father!'

Another terrible irony! It is as if it were expected that a Communist father would have a Communist child. And history made it quite clear that many of the children of Communist Party workers had joined a violent organization like the Shiv Sena.

'Everyone calls him the Communist son-in-law.'

'He gets magazines and money from Russia.'

It was actually the Black Panthers from America who were sending him their newsletters.

'He's bought a house in Bandra for eighty thousand rupees.'

'He has Lenin and Marx up on his walls. No photograph of Ambedkar at all.'

'He's shaking hands with Brezhnev in a photograph.' (In reality that was a photograph of him shaking hands with Castro.)

It should be clear from this how much suspicion and bitterness the Dalit people felt for the Communists and their ideology. But on the other hand, the young Dalit Panthers, who had no commitment and ideological position, were simply going astray. They knew nothing other than to take out morchas and shout slogans and make speeches. They knew nothing of Ambedkar's thought nor did they see that an organization needs discipline and an ideological framework. Everything was there on paper. They had no idea that simply abusing those you saw as opponents was not going to frighten them off, nor was it going to make them bow down in defeat. They did not see the need to study the political systems of the world, to do their homework about world politics and to catch the opponents on precise points. Even today, they seek to become leaders instantly. To them, politics was a matter of fun and games, something that should not take time.

Namdeo, too, was floundering. He was being hurt all the time. He was watching the organization he had built up fall apart. He was surrounded by criticism and accusations. Each day, he came home reading, 'Dhasal dhaasalla' (Dhasal has bit the dirt), a cruel pun on his name. He was banned from Worli Camp[47] and he would see this slogan again and again each time he went there.

He had to bear these people's gazes poisoned with suspicion, he had to listen to their sarcastic remarks and bear witness to the distrust and despair of the youth. At this time he had people like Arjun Dangle, Bal Khairmode, Chendwankar and Sunil Dighe with him, but they were not full-time workers. They had other jobs and worked with the movement as well. They were sincere but not really in politics, except for Sunil Dighe.

There was no chance of getting funds. But whatever happened, I had decided that I was not going home. (Running home to Mother is a time-honoured practice among women.) I was fully absorbed in my new life. Even this bitter experience brought its own joys. We supported each other in these times, looked out for each other. I might not have understood every aspect of his situation but even so I wasn't questioning him. I was getting my two meals a day. He was not without

---

[47]This refers to Worli Labour Camp, a Dalit stronghold and one of the epicentres of the riots.

hope. He could not see himself giving it all up, admitting defeat and accepting the stability of a job. Each day, he would somehow manage to scrape together ten to fifteen rupees and come home with that. I tried to understand what was going on but I could see no way out. I simply trusted Namdeo.

~

We went to Pune. He would hold two meetings a day and then come back to the lodge where we were living. In Pune, he had built up a strong organization. There was no privacy in the lodge. He was never alone. And I was used to being alone. Chandu, his right-hand man, would also come to sleep in the lodge. This would annoy me. To have someone sleep next to one's husband, that too when one was a newly-wed? Finally, Chandu began to sleep in the corridor. Namdeo would return late after the meetings and there would always be people with him. We would only get to sleep at one or two o'clock. By seven or eight in the morning, they would be up again. That would irritate me. These people would be with him all day. Their jokes, discussions, conversations, stories and meals made it difficult for me even to change my clothes. It always surprised me how our political leaders, who do not have steady jobs, get married and, having no visible source of income, are expected to feed everyone around them, even when these people lived quite close by.

They did not seem to feel that they should give us, a newly married couple, some time to ourselves. Namdeo would forget all about me and immerse himself in their company. This infuriated me. I would signal to him and only then would he tell them to leave. Those early days, which should have been lovely for me, were ruined and so I have dislike for the city.

~

Regardless of how well we knew our guests or how little, I always made tea for them. But how was I to feed random guests brought home without warning? But then Namdeo had a very different idea about the best way to build an organization.

From the moment I entered Pune, I was warmly welcomed as Namdeo's wife. The women in the basti performed an aarti, they raised slogans in my name. They praised my singing. This elevation got under my skin.

And in the middle of all this, some money disappeared from Namdeo's wallet. He was calm, as if nothing had happened. He hunted a bit and that was it. That evening there was a Panthers' meeting. It was a public event. We needed money to pay for the lodge, for dinner, for travel. Namdeo asked for a three- or four-tola gold necklace which my father had had made for me. I took it off and gave it to him. He took it to the pawnshop immediately. I received much praise for my sacrifice. But I grew a little thoughtful, a little solemn. I had no great love of gold; that wasn't it. But my father had made that necklace for me. That was my sentimental value for it.

We returned from Pune.

~

I stopped taking the birth-control pills because they didn't agree with me. Our sexual life was going well and soon I felt that…or rather, I suspected something. A visit to the doctor confirmed my suspicions. I was pregnant.

When Namdeo came home that evening, there was no electricity. The candles were lit. I coyly broke the news to him. He hugged me, delighted. He kissed me on the cheek. Then he ran out and leaped about telling Latif-bhaiyya, 'Arré, I'm going to be a father.'

I was also thrilled.

Before this, Namdeo had organized a fifteen-day study circle. Selected people had been invited. Many well-known thinkers were called to speak. The sponsor pulled out at the last moment. Now what? How were we to pay for fifteen people over fifteen days? I took off my two gold bangles and my earrings and gave them quietly to Namdeo. Now I was innocent of all jewellery but the study circle could proceed. And it was these people who stood by Namdeo later.

~

Namdeo's mother was one of the pillars of the movement. She had spent countless days and nights cooking. Whether it was people she knew or people who had suddenly turned up, she had served them all, often not eating herself so that others might eat well. I often said to Namdeo, 'You lot took advantage of her illiteracy. She cooked for all of you and you exploited her. She had to work day and night while you went about making speeches. You must be the first to start an organization in this manner. Do other people start organizations like this?'

However, it must be said that Namdeo's mother loved to cook for these people. Were they not giving her son love and attention? How could she send them off without a meal?

I would ask angrily: 'But will you not think about tomorrow?'

But Namdeo's mother remained naive and loving right up to the end. She never behaved to me as a stereotypical mother-in-law is supposed to behave. I could never figure her out either. All her life, she had been long-suffering and accommodating but what had she gained from it?

~

This is a story from the time before Namdeo was born. Namdeo's father had a great love of the tamasha and equally an eye for the women. One day, he brought home a young woman from the tamasha. What do you think his wife did? She welcomed them into the house and went out, locking the door so that they might not be disturbed. When her sister-in-law came with the water, she said, 'Hold on a bit, he's in there.'

Her sister-in-law was shocked to hear this.

How does this fit in with the dharma of a woman, with her character? What mould had she been made from? I had never heard of a woman who would help her husband have it off with another woman.

~

Namdeo and I had gone to Pune. His mother and father were at home. After about fifteen days, we got the news that his mother was ill and that her brain had been affected. We came back. For the next fortnight, she terrified us. Someone had told her—and to this day I do not know who it was—that Namdeo and I had been killed.

That unhinged her mind. She began to babble incoherently. She would slam her head on the walls. She would fling herself off the cot and on to the floor. There was a creek below the chawl. She got down into it to look for Namdeo. There was a tattered old shirt there which she took hold of and began to weep and wail. Nobody could control her. My mother got to hear about this. She brought Namdeo's mother home but it was difficult to get through to her.

She was brought to Bandra. When we got there, nothing changed. Even if Namdeo were in front of her, she would continue to babble and moan. And from time to time, she'd get up and make a dash for it. Namdeo sent her off to the village but she only got worse there. She began to run into the jungle, ripping her flesh on thorn bushes. She would jump on to tawas that were hot on the griddle. She would grab live coals with her hands and no marks appeared on them. Her brother was the village exorcist. He thought she was possessed—and wanted to try an exorcism. Namdeo was furious. He went and brought his mother home immediately. He had an old grudge against his uncle. This man's eldest son had tuberculosis. His father had tried to cure him with village remedies. What need did he have for medicines and doctors? The disease raged on. And the father's exorcisms kept pace in fury. He would tie his son to a post and whip him and in the end, the boy died.

Namdeo's mother too would have visitations from Mari-aai but her son was having none of this. So he warned her: 'Look, Aai, I don't know all this Mari-aai thing (and here you should insert a juicy Marathi cussword of your choice) but if she comes back, let me tell you, I'm going to go to the railway tracks and kill myself.'

Mari-aai vanished, never to return, but the naïve mother remained.

Namdeo was a child who had been much prayed

for. He was supposed to be a gift from Lord Shankar. His parents were believers and observed all the rituals and festivals. After learning a little about Communism, Namdeo stopped all this—no celebrations, no rituals, no festival observances. He would insist on puran poli being made on days other than when it was traditionally made, certainly not on Pola and Nag Panchami. His parents gave up on him, this child they had prayed for to the gods he wanted them to abandon.

In the middle of this attack, I took her to Dr Patkar[48] of Nair Hospital. When I went to make the case paper, she hopped up and ran away. I was alone. It was difficult to control her. Finally, she was given some pills and we brought her home. After just two weeks of drugs, she returned to normal. We were all relieved and happy.

'Arré, your daughter-in-law cured you,' Namdeo told her.

The poor thing smiled affectionately and gently stroked my head.

~

My pregnancy was going fine. I was so happy that it was difficult to contain it and everyone found out. Even in that condition, I would finish all the work and go for meetings afterwards. We would have many fights which

---

[48]Dr A. P. Patkar was the head of the Department of Psychiatry between 1982 and 1992.

would end in my weeping. Then he would pacify me, console me, and I would melt and forget everything as I dried my tears in his arms. It was also during this time that, annoyed over something, he slapped me. The images of togetherness, of family life I had nourished, were destroyed. I wept in pain, I wept for the end of my dreams and in the end, he was unhappy that he had hit me.

At that time, I went home infrequently. I wasn't one to make a big difference between my marital home and my maternal home. Perhaps because I had a father complex, I was attached to Namdeo; he was like a father figure to me. I needed to be in love with somebody, ferociously in love.

~

When Didi had a daughter, I was in Pune. I could not go for some reason and so both were annoyed with me. Then Namdeo said something about Didi, about my family, and the two of them fought and cursed each other.

In the middle of all this, we continued to live in Pune, far away. Namdeo's aunt would criticize and taunt me whenever she got the opportunity. I took nothing lying down, not then, not now. I was somewhat egoistic too. I refused to bow down before anyone. And before these illiterate women? Their behaviour, their conversation, the topics they chose, what was I to say to them?

Namdeo had his meetings, his workers, his sabhas. I was terribly lonely. And that in turn made me angry. And so I quietly took some of the pills that had been prescribed for Aai. And left for Anil-bhaiyya's home. When the rickshaw crossed Lakdi Pul, my body felt heavy, my eyes began to close, my head began to spin. Somehow, I made it to their home and fell on the bed and went to sleep. Fortunately, they didn't ask any questions.

~

Whenever Namdeo and I had a fight, I would bear the brunt of it, and carry the tension inside my head. When he said something cruel, it would echo in my head for days. I would go blank and then try to kill myself. This was an extreme reaction. It was difficult to justify or to confess or even to deny. It was all very difficult. But one thing is true. Even during those times of pain and sorrow, I wanted to live. In fact, I knew that this much was not going to kill me. One's subconscious mind is always at work, they say. And as if by an invisible and silent force, it would be constantly dragging me back. Or it was as if a telephone bell was ringing and I was telling myself I should ignore it but I could not. I was completely out of control and at the same time, a great alertness, a great cautiousness would also surface. Yet my mind was slowly freezing over. I felt as if I had suffered an internal short circuit. This would happen very often. And then I would sleep soundly. I was aware of something changing in my personality, an imperceptible, cautious, hesitant change. But a change nonetheless, a change within and without.

7

Our time in Bandra was coming to an end. It had never been a home. At that very moment, Anil-bhaiyya and Didi had a fight with Aai and moved out. He had taken an office in Dadar for the monthly magazine *Vidroh* (Rebellion) and they began to stay there. It was a single room with no bathroom and no water supply. They kept their daughter Phulwa somewhere she would be looked after. There were many problems. Didi was going to end up ill, I knew. But she had always been accommodating and efficient. After marriage, she became reserved. As for me, I would shout a lot and weep buckets and make scenes. But during the rest of the time, I would be full of enthusiasm and energy. In Bandra, we had been very poor. No money was coming Namdeo's way. Our caste folks had trapped us. There was gossip and rumour rampant. There was confusion and there was romantic revolutionary zeal; there was anarchy and no discipline to control it.

And yet there would be people to feed. Often I would mumble and mutter about this but Namdeo paid no attention. When we ran out of rations, I would make a nice big pile of *Soviet Land* magazines and sell them. From the proceeds, I would buy tea, sugar, wheat and the other necessities of life. That is how the Communist Party and the Communist countries often came to our aid.

Everyone got involved in our fights. We would begin with a civilized critique of each other but the middlemen who were always present would magnify these fights and turn them into something quite different. Because of the volume and scope of this interference, we would often end up derailed.

Once in a while, when the party workers were debating something, we would go into the other room and work out a compromise and fall into each other's arms. Latif-bhaiyya was often a witness to all this. He was a teacher. But even so, everything from the soles of his shoes to the cloth of his trousers to the price of the prostitutes he visited was borne by Namdeo. I would get very angry with him. He was always with us when times were good. He always spoke sweetly. But he never put a hand into his pocket. Once we had to pawn the copper vessels and brass buckets but though he had his salary he had no money to loan us. One would think that after eating and drinking at Namdeo's expense, he might offer some help but when we were down and out, he would simply stop coming. This was how I learned the truth about human nature. It seems that Namdeo had relatives without number, all of whom felt entitled to a meal. It never failed to astonish me how these people could eat so happily at the home of a man who had no job and whose house was running on nothing. Once they arrived only Brahma in his wisdom knew when they would choose to leave again. I had no use for relatives like these. Namdeo did not like to visit them either. If at all he went, it was clear that he was not comfortable. He hated me to go and stay anywhere else. The restrictions on our relationship were beginning to prove painful.

~

Once Namdeo wrote a street play, a political satire. I had many contacts in theatre and some knowledge of it that he could use. But the Emergency was on. Over and above, the workers who had come from Pune to take part in the play fled when they saw our poverty-stricken state. We did not have enough money to eat. How were we to stage a play?

Namdeo was in the habit of using taxis to go wherever

he wanted. So if he had a hundred rupees, sixty would be spent on a cab and the rest was left for us.

If he got hold of two or three hundred rupees, he'd spend a hundred on books. I would sit with my head in my hands. No kerosene in the house, no provisions in the kitchen; could we eat books?

He would sit and read. I would lie next to him and when the baby kicked I would guide his hand to my stomach. He would laugh proudly. I did not suffer much during my pregnancy. The only thing I had a craving for was mangoes. I could eat six or seven a day. My cheeks swelled up. I put on a little weight.

~

A memory from the rains. I had gone to the Saat Rasta house. Namdeo came there and we went to see the film *Aavishkar* at the Plaza Cinema.

When the film got over and we emerged from the theatre, the rains had taken over the reins of the city. The buses, the taxis, even the trucks, had been rendered immobile. The water was up to our knees. A biting wind was lashing the streets. We had no umbrellas, no protection of any kind. Finally, we began to walk but by the time we got to Dadar TT,[49] the water was up to my

[49]TT refers to Tram Terminus. Mumbai was once a tram city. Now the place is known as Khodadad Circle but old names die hard.

thighs. I was terrified. How were we to go forward? I was in the third day of my periods. Namdeo was holding me tight, lest I slip. I was shivering. My sari was drenched through. The water was now at my hips. Ugh. Everything was disgusting. I was soaked to the skin.

We managed to get to the Wadala Hostel.[50] They didn't want to let me in because it was a boys' hostel. Namdeo had to shout and curse and make a huge row before we were given shelter. The boys emptied a room for us. It was difficult to think of taking off one's clothes so I tried unsuccessfully to sleep in my wet clothes. I was hungry too. The next morning, we got up early and left. The water had not receded. The transport systems were still not functional. A few trucks waded slowly through the water. We walked for hours until we got a ride in a truck. Then a bus. Finally, when we reached Saat Rasta, we found that the rain had flooded the area. The flood waters would have certainly entered our home. I thumped my head in disgust. I wanted to throw my clothes and my body into the water. We turned right around and went to Bhai Sangare's[51] house. I gave up all embarrassment and simply asked his wife for a change of clothes. She was a good woman. She gave me a sari and everything else I

---

[50]This may refer to Siddharth Vihar, a hostel for Dalit boys.

[51]Bhai Sangare (?-1999), activist, orator, writer and thinker, died when he was enveloped in fire as he tried to burn a copy of the *Manusmriti* in public.

needed. By then Namdeo had gone home, swimming half the way. Since the water had entered the ground floor, everyone had taken shelter on the first floor. Namdeo counted his money. He bought bread for fifty rupees and four or five dozen bananas and gave it to them. Then he came back. I developed a fever after that. That memory will not fade.

8

We came back to Saat Rasta, lugging such worldly goods as we had. The housing board was repairing the building. The house was now open to the sky because the roof had been taken off. There was no electricity or gas, no water. There was mud and dust and building material everywhere. I was now close to delivery. My body grew heavy but I kept working hard. Out of fear, really. I had heard that if you kept busy, if you exercised, delivering a baby would be easier. And so I cooked, I cleaned, I washed, all the while protecting my tummy.

And one day, a fine pain began in my stomach. I woke Aai up and she had a bath and took me to Nair Hospital. I was frightened, my forehead wet with sweat. The nurses looked at me without feeling.

'How many you had?' one asked in Hindi.

'This is my first.'

The doctor came along.

'I want an operation. I can't bear too much pain.'

She laughed.

'Why are you frightened? Natural childbirth is the best.'

I could not bear pain. Each contraction now seemed to set my body on fire. It seemed as if the muscles of my waist and hips were being mangled. When each subsided, I would fall into an exhausted sleep until the next pang would rouse me from my half-conscious state. I began to howl. I was surrounded by women close to delivery. They were calmly waiting for the moment of their release. The ayahs would make lewd jokes. Even in that state, I wanted to stick a gun into the mouth of one of them as they mocked the pain of other women.

With a contemptuous laugh, one would say: 'Now you're crying. How did it feel when you were taking it in?' and comments of the sort.

Pain. More pain. Only pain.

My throat dried up. The pain increased. I was no longer aware of whether I was dressed or not. My body was now all pain. And yet, hardly any time had passed. 8:30 a.m. to 9:30 a.m. One hour. Just one hour. It seemed like an aeon of suffering.

Finally, it was time. Four or five nurses advanced upon

me, carrying instruments. Now I was a dead duck who no longer fears the fire. 'Do what you want,' I thought, 'just stop this agony.'

'That's it. Push now. Don't go to sleep. Hey, are you sleeping?'

I was only half-conscious in this haze of pain. And I was tired. My body felt as if it had been squeezed in a mangle. At one point I was about to fall off the gurney when a nurse saved me. This annoyed them as if it were my fault.

I lay there, my thighs wide open, my calves splayed. Ward-boys were coming and going but instead of feeling shame, I was only afraid that I might die. If this was supposed to be the height of fulfilment of femininity, I had nothing to say; I only wanted to spit at it. Someone thrust my knees up to my stomach and held them there. They cut me down there. In this symphony of pain, this was a new high note on which the new life pushed its way out. The nurse put it in a tub and showed it to me. It was all red, a raw piece of flesh, the umbilical cord still attached, the birth blood smeared over it. I took one look and blurted out:

'What is it?'

'A boy.'

I was disappointed. The nurse was shocked. Here I had got myself a boy on my first time out and I was not over the moon.

'It's a boy!'

She seemed much more excited that I was. Neither Namdeo nor I had any preferences as to the gender of our child. We had both seen my pregnancy as a natural process by which another human being would be born. An addition to the eighteen per minute that were being born all over the planet. Love and nurturing and all the rest of that would come later.

At home, they got the news. Namdeo came to see me in the evening. He was obviously full of pride and curiosity about his son. When his aunt went to pick up the baby, he scolded her sharply: 'Don't touch him.'

I wanted to laugh.

The hospital experience was boring in the extreme, the boredom punctuated by moans and sighs and groans. Here, the world seemed sick and old, with ayahs and ward-boys as its unacknowledged legislators. Or perhaps this was a different world altogether. On the first day, I was dry. The next day, the milk came but it was thick. Perhaps because it was too thick or insufficient, the hospital mixed it with glucose solution. The baby would cry. Because of the stitches, I could not move. No one paid any attention. This was the nurses' job but they were too busy talking among themselves or chatting up the doctors to bother. Or they just weren't there.

The maternity ward also had its resident mad woman.

She just would not go home and occupied one of the beds. She was generally all right but when the fit was upon her, she would scream and wail and attack people. Then the nurses would seize her and tie her to a cot. She would continue to keen and shriek. I was seized with the dread that she might get hold of my baby. The whole atmosphere of that ward was of bitter sadness. So must a jail feel.

At 4 p.m., the ward would come alive with men and visitors. Some would be delighted, some downcast at the birth of a fifth girl. But what had the sparrow-lives, sleeping so peacefully in their cradles, to do with all this fuss? They would sometimes condescend to wave their closed fists at the visitors, as if asking, 'What do you think I have in my pink fist?'

At 6 p.m., again that deathlike quiet would descend. Now the pills would make the rounds. The faces of the women would sag in tiredness. The air would admit defeat, filling with the sound of infants crying. The stitches made even movement difficult. The ayahs would get irritated if we asked for a bedpan or if we asked them to bring our children from the cradle. They would rumble and mumble curses under their breaths.

Then the lady doctor came and gave me an injection and began to stitch me up. With her was a man whom I assumed was another doctor though he did not have a white coat on. He must have been an assistant doctor, or at least I hoped he was. He was standing next to her and chatting all the while as she stitched up my genitals. I was dying of shame but in that horrific general ward, I learned one more truth: physical pain is the worst thing in the world. No one else suffers your pain. You alone understand its magnitude and intensity. Each time pain wracks you, your nerves demoralize you; your soul weakens a little more. This is a world of suffering alone. Shame and modesty have no part to play here. But I did I felt a little better after that, as if I were being cleaned, purified.

The feeling did not last. The bathrooms were filthy. One went there only because there was no other option, covering one's eyes, holding one's nose in one's fist.

This is where women come again and again? To undergo this death? My hair stood on end at the thought. This was where they ensured the posterity of their families? Where they first experienced the joy of motherhood? Where femininity reached its apogee?

Yuck.

Should women accept these euphemisms that have been obviously invented by men? Should we not question them? What happiness can a woman find in such suffering? Why should she be lured down unfamiliar paths, paths that lead nowhere? Why must she content herself with fine shining promises that will never be fulfilled? This world terrified me. Even its empty peace had the same quality of hovering between life and death. In that world of sighs and groans, I made up my mind: I was not coming back.

I came home. Namdeo was in high spirits. He appeared to be very far away from me. Or had I moved away from him? My needs, my existence and its joys had been erased from his life. This hurt me deeply. Far more than a child, I needed a husband, a companion in those days. Namdeo had no enthusiasm for family life.

Aai had to do everything. He came and went as he always did; early or late, it made no difference to him. It did not occur to him to buy anything for the newborn. He went to Delhi and other places, leaving a contact number for emergencies. If anything, his travelling increased. He said nothing about the world outside. He did not sit down next to me to talk nor did he play with his newborn son. Conversation between us dwindled.

One day, the baby had a sore mouth. He would not drink. Namdeo was not at home. I called Dr Anand. When the doctor was examining the sick baby, Namdeo came home. He did not have the time to stop and even look.

'I'm off,' he said and left immediately. I could see that the doctor found his behaviour astonishing. I felt a deep pain in my heart. Two days later, Namdeo left for Delhi. I hated it when he left town. I would count the hours to his return. When a taxi stopped in the street outside, my heart would thunder and I would be beside myself with happiness.

Then Namdeo came back from Delhi and announced his support of the Emergency.

Now he had no time to talk to me, no time to tell me of the ups and downs of his political life.

I learned of these things from other people. Namdeo was also drinking much more than he did earlier. While my body was trying to repair itself, my mind was full of tension.

And then Didi was preparing to return to live with us. She decided to partition the room. She wanted to have the bathroom on her side. But Namdeo, his bath, the never-ending stream of workers, this would increase the tension in the house and so a new bathroom was built. A strange discomfort erupted in my mind. I had known such happy days in this house.

And now it was to be divided into two. This was, I reasoned, because of Namdeo. There were omens, unholy signs that began to appear. Something was going to happen, something unpleasant. This fear began to haunt me. Namdeo was drinking anyway, he paid no attention to the house. He came and went as he pleased, always with someone or the other. It was difficult to talk to him when there were strangers present.

And Didi was also there. But I was slowly drifting away from everyone. I was aware of that. The poems weren't coming either. Money came into the house and went again but it didn't pass through my hands. He gave me none, unless it was just to keep for a while. I had no idea where it had come from, who had given it to him or where it went again. I was now completely immersed in home and the baby. We had fights but I could not let myself scream and cry. To do so would be to demonstrate to Didi and Anil-bhaiyya, who were just across the wall, the collapse of the world I was supposed to have created. That would be the equivalent of death. Namdeo's sister and her husband came to stay. She took over the burden of cooking and the household chores.

~

Neither of us was much in favour of having a naming ceremony. But on the day we built his cradle and decorated it with flowers and laid him down in it. I named him Ashutosh. Namdeo had suggested George Jackson and other revolutionary names like that.

~

We fought. We fought about his drinking. We fought over his uncontrolled spending. We fought about him bringing party workers home for meals. We fought over his foul language and ugly behaviour. We fought over the strangers who dropped in—and had to be fed and watered. I got angry but he couldn't care less. Rations?

He would get a whole sack of wheat. Once he spent eight hundred rupees only on spices.[52] He never had the faintest idea of how to spend money. But he could not find it in himself to ask me either. Nor did he give me money. All the clothes and toys for Ashutosh had been given to him by my friends and family.

Every day a new experience: some bitter, some sweet.

~

He began to spend more time outside the house. He would stay out until two or three in the morning. If I asked him where he had been, he would beat me. The tears would follow.

One night, he came home drunk and demanded that I get up. He abused me once again. Something snapped in me and I got up and hit him across the face. He hit me back and then muttering to himself, he went off to sleep. Exhausted, I went to sleep too. I just could not look after Ashu. I was bored out of my mind, sitting at home. I had never been confined to the house for such a long period of time.

~

---

[52]In 1975, the value of the Indian rupee was pegged at 8.39 against a dollar. That means Namdeo spent the equivalent of nearly a hundred dollars on spices. This is not a good estimate, I know, but it means about Rs 5,000 worth of spices today.

And so a vicious cycle began: drinking, fighting, abusing, beating. But of all these sorrows, the greatest was this: I had lost my Namdeo, the Namdeo of old. He was changing, drifting away from me, and there was nothing I could do to stop it. I had loved his companionship but he felt no need for me now. This bitter truth broke something inside me.

And as if this was not enough, I heard a rumour that shattered me completely.

Someone was always with him. Privacy was impossible in our house. And then one of Namdeo's relatives came to stay with us. He was smart, slim and a wastrel. He would drink and get into trouble. There wasn't just a plywood partition now between Didi and me; there was now a powerful poisonous fog. We were trying to keep the relationship alive but it was an artificial attempt. There was a suspicious wariness on both sides. This had been caused by the Namdeo and Anil equation. The young man would drink and tell lies about Namdeo to Anil-bhaiyya. Then he would gossip to Namdeo about Didi and Anil-bhaiyya.

He sowed seeds of suspicion and discord. And I had to reap the bitter harvest.

One day I found out the truth about him: that he had been spreading lies about us and about them. I flew into a rage and picking up a heavy volume that was to hand, I threw it at him and drove him away.

But the tension did not decrease; it just kept growing. A young woman turned up for a job with Air India. She was fair and pretty. While she was waiting for the call, Namdeo decided to 'interview' her himself. The two of them began to go around together. Once they went to Pune and had a great time.

Namdeo had not said a word about where he was going so I was frantic with worry. I could not even pay attention to my child. I could not eat or drink. I called every number I knew. I wandered about, looking for him in the oddest of places. Even as I write this today, I feel the shame and anger of those days coming back. I was losing something and trying to cling to it. My head was heavy, my nerves shredded. I was always on the verge of tears. I felt such a terrible degree of helplessness, such a loss of dignity.

After he returned, we went through the usual reassurances, consolations, protestations of innocence et cetera. But when I later went to Pune, one of the women of the family told me details about the affair only because Namdeo had told her of an affair that her husband had had, which led to a huge fight between the husband and wife. This was her revenge. Everyone, it seemed, was playing games.

And so I understood what he was doing—this was the first shock of my life. I was so hurt by this that I spent the next two months in tears.

No, the next year was spent in a haze of pain and sadness. I had sacrificed everything to be with this man. My health deteriorated and I have not recovered, even today. My nerves still feel taut, the blood still rushes into my eyes. That he should cheat on me was a thought too terrible to contemplate. How could he have descended to this level? Neither I nor my love was so cheap. I lost interest in food.

And because I would not eat, the fights began again. One night, when Ashu was eight months old, Namdeo picked him up and walked out of the house. I was lying on the bed, stanching the flow of blood from my nose for he had just finished with hitting me. I did not feel like allowing even those close to me to approach. My mind, my body, my spirit, were devastated. Each moment was like death. What was his relationship with Ashu? He had had his moment of pleasure when he had sown his seed. I had borne the child for nine months inside my body. I had suffered the death agonies of childbirth. And yet he felt he had the right to drag my child from me and walk out. How was that possible? I had no strength left to think. I was numb. Through that night, my mind spun on its own axis, like a top. I could not see myself staying here, like this. I could not see my way to moving on. My eyes were too swollen to shut. Every road seemed closed to me. Time stood still. The night stood still.

At dawn, around 6 or 7 a.m., he brought Ashu home. The child was hungry and had caught a cold. As soon as I saw Ashu, my exhaustion dropped away and I decided to end the relationship. I hid my books and my vessels, things I had bought with such expectation. Out of our dreams come these desires to hoard and to gather. I left and went to Lonavla. The next night, at 2 a.m., the phone rang. It was Didi.

She was in a fine rage. Namdeo had returned and had raised hell. He had cursed and abused them roundly. 'You've stolen my wife,' he had screamed. Didi told me that I had to return immediately and I did. Namdeo had left and was at Latif-bhaiyya's Andheri flat. I got there by 8 a.m. and who should I find there but the fair flighty air hostess? But what relationship did we have left that I should object to this affair of his? He saw me and smiled and tried his usual tactics.

I was having none of that. 'Give me all the trouble you want. I can take it. I'm still strong. But leave my family alone. Don't you come back to Saat Rasta and start fights for no reason. No physical stuff. We can separate amicably, don't you think, without hurting each other any further?'

He took my hand and sat me down. He despatched the girl. He swore solemn oaths. He begged my pardon and touched my feet. He explained, he cajoled, he pleaded and then Ashu came and hugged me. His innocent gaze melted my resolve and I compromised again.

For a few months, things went well. And then we were back where we started: the alcohol, the beatings, the abusive language and all the rest of it. One evening, he took me out for a walk with L. D. Bhosale[53] to Dadar. It was about 10 or 10.30 p.m. 'Back in a minute,' he said and vanished for an hour. I got angry. It was not a very good part of Dadar and it was soon 11 p.m. LD was a nice man but if it came to that, he wasn't going to be much good in a fight. And the boys began to gather:

'How about it?' one asked.

'Coming with me?' another asked.

I was so outraged that I caught a cab and went home to Andheri. There my mother-in-law asked me, 'Where's he?'

'He'll come.'

'You left him alone and came?'

This was salt on my wounds.

'Your son is not a child. He left me in the middle of the street, in the night, and you're worried about him? He spent twenty-five years of his life pushing people around in a neighbourhood full of thugs and hoods. What's going to happen to him? He's used to wandering about in the night.'

Namdeo was not going to change. Was I going to spend my life waiting for some magical transformation? I picked up my bag. Ashu began to cry. He was a healthy

---

[53]L. D. Bhosale was the leader of the Dalit Panthers in Pune.

child, with big eyes that were without sin and without guile. He raised his chubby arms to me, pleading with me. Arré deva! Why had I accepted this maternal role? What curse was this?

But were I to have stayed and endured, I would have had to endure even more. So I averted my eyes and steeled myself. What was I thinking? My physical strength was sapped. My mind was half-dead, stained in blood, cut in pieces. I turned my back on all that. I banished my own child from my life. But what could I do? Namdeo would never give him to me. He felt no compassion for me at all.

When I left I went to Dada, Bhai's friend. Aai came there too. I told her: 'I'm not feeling well. Take me somewhere for a change of air.'

We fixed on Kolhapur. R. V. Patil, one of Bhai's friends, lived there. Whenever we had holidays as children, we would visit them.

Aai brought me to Kolhapur and went back. I did not tell her that I had fought with Namdeo and left him. I confided everything in Bai (Mrs Patil). She consoled me and encouraged me. And slowly, in their crowded bungalow, I began to heal again. Good meals, some outings, visits to the pictures… Mrs Patil treated me as if I were her own daughter.

I remembered something my sister had said to me: 'If you choose to go back to him, you'll have to look after yourself. We will not be able to protect you.'

I started to attend a typing class in Kolhapur. And then I went to Bai's daughter in Goa.

I wandered around Goa a great deal. Nature was soothing and beautiful, reaching into me to heal me. Everyone fussed over me and tried to get me to eat. But memories of Ashu would haunt me.

I got a long screed from Namdeo, addressed to Kolhapur.

'Let us stop fighting. I will control my ego and set it aside. At least come back for Ashu's sake...Please forgive me...I admit that I was wrong...I promise never to treat you badly again.'

And much more of the same.

I sent him back a stern reply.

A few days later, I was back in Saat Rasta.

~

If I gathered all the letters I had written him from the time of our marriage to the present, they would fill a book. He came to see me at Saat Rasta. I was silent.

He returned. He begged and pleaded. He brought Ashutosh with him on another occasion. Ashutosh did not recognize me. That hurt. He came again.

And finally, I went with him to Andheri.

After we stayed a year in Andheri, there was a suggestion that we move in with Latif-bhaiyya, but after much discussion we went to Lonavla instead. I had written a number of poems. There was now a goodly number of them. Our economic state was still uncertain. But as always, there were still people coming and going in the house.

People we'd met only the day before would walk straight into the kitchen.

I had no political knowledge nor had I studied much. But seeing how the savants destroy everything they touch, I did not think I was missing much. My poetry somehow continued to reflect my social awareness.

Namdeo's political manoeuvres had completely failed. He had ideas, he had done his homework, he had good oratorical skills, he could write well but, despite all this, he was destroying himself, from a political point of view. He would go where he could find money. He was an opportunist. He had great connections with policemen and goondas. But his community looked upon him as a Communist and criticized him for being one. He succeeded for a while, and relished the taste of success, but all too soon failure followed and frustration came with it. And these things changed him completely.

~

I remember the time I would go to meet him in jail during the whirlwind days of the Panther movement. I would carry a dabba of food and stand at the door of the court. I would be looking for ways to make bail for him.

I failed at my attempts to rescue him. There was no point telling him anything.

'What do you know about that? What's it to you anyway?' he would snap and silence me. Thousands of rupees would come in but they would be spent on bottles of liquor, taxis across the city and meals at expensive restaurants. I would get angry and we would fight.

I could see how his friends and his family were taking advantage of him and I began to hate them for this. He had nothing to do with the home. Decorating the house, making it look a little better…these were bourgeois dreams, according to him.

'And eating at the Sun 'n' Sand hotel, smoking cigars and drinking expensive liquor, taking taxis everywhere, is that how the revolutionary should behave? Or are those the ways of the lumpen proletariat? A little money for one's child in a bank, buying a few nice things for the house, that's bourgeois for you? Such convenient logic,' I would retort.

From the money left after shopping, from the money he gave me to keep, I bought some pillows, cushions and curtains for the house. This annoyed him but then he would enjoy these things as much as anyone else.

~

So we went to Lonavla, as I said. There was a nice spacious room in the Railway quarters that someone had given us.

This man was a bachelor and so here, too, I had no help with the housework. It drove me mad. I could not see myself as the complete housewife. All day I had to be hard at it: the cleaning, the washing and the cooking. How was I to get any time to myself? And the house was isolated. I could not go chatter with the other women of the chawl; I was simply not built that way. Namdeo was out all the time. I was alone with Ashu in the house, alone with the ghost of my loneliness. I grew desperate. And then Namdeo, who had his fair share of bad habits, decided to add a new one. He would leave for Pune, saying, 'Home tomorrow' and vanish for weeks at a time. There was no money—and then those people who came to eat as if by right would disappear when I needed them.

The man whose house it was, the bachelor, also lived there. He was a man of military discipline; everyone was scared of him. He was a die-hard Republican, Ambedkarite, et cetera. In many ways he was progressive, but in the matter of women? Just to pass time, I would sit and argue with him. Or rather fight with him. He would get irritated. Here I was, a rent-payer, a woman, in his house, giving him the benefit of my 'extraordinary opinions'? This was too much. He was forever citing Sita and other examples from mythology. I would reply:

'Oh, that's wonderful. You're using the very scriptures that turned you into an untouchable, that put you into the lowest category of humanity, that treated you as if you were an animal, as examples to me? So do you want women to sacrifice ourselves? In your speeches you deride Hindu mythology but, in your own home, you seek to victimize women by using the example of Sita?'

He would end up confused and annoyed.

One of the faceless masses who turned up to eat included Ranga, one of the numberless relatives of Namdeo. He, at least, would try and help. But the brahmachari bachelor and Namdeo so harassed him that he too vanished.

Once, Namdeo was in Pune. There was not a paisa in the house. And I began to suffer an unclean pain that just would not go away. On both sides of my pubic area, boils erupted. Pus began to form inside. The pain got worse but who could I tell? I knew no one in the area. There was a doctor in the village but I had no money for his fees. I was beginning to feel dizzy almost every other minute. I had no energy. I began to run a fever and lose weight. I recognized the symptoms. This was one of the gifts Namdeo had given me, a souvenir of his days with prostitutes. My body filled me with revulsion now. How carefully I had looked after it. How carefully I had washed and dried myself. When it was possible, I would take a bath before sleeping with Namdeo, for I had felt that one's body must be clean and beautiful for the person one loves. And now? What should I feel for Namdeo? I wanted to gash and score him with my nails. I wanted to empty an entire revolver-barrel of bullets into his chest. What right had he to play with my life? Was my love my only crime?

Finally, the dizziness got so bad, I began to fall over. Doing the housework became impossible. Just sitting down to cut an onion was agony. I put aside my shame and called Babu's 'wife'. 'Wife' because they had never really married but she was accepted as if she were his wife. She was small, dark, thinner than me and a lovely person, affectionate and peaceful. She was a railway-station sweeper.

She gave me some money and took me to a doctor. He was a young man—and I died another death. I could not raise my eyes to his, I had not the courage. I told him the name of the injection that I needed and he looked at me for a long moment and then gave it to me.

~

Namdeo came back from Pune. We had a huge fight. There were scenes, tears, recriminations. Out of the darkness, I wrote to my mother: 'I find it difficult to manage here. There's no room. I'm coming back.'

In the meanwhile, Didi and Anil-bhaiyya had had a fight with Aai. She was of a somewhat difficult temperament and when she could not get on with her first-born child, how could anyone expect her to deal well with her stay-at-home son-in-law? Didi found another place and left. Aai was now alone. I could not deal with her pain. Each person seems to have a share of pain to deal with. How is anyone else to understand? Trying to share it or to support the person, to take sides even, is quite false.

Intellectually, she could understand Communist ideology but her heart was not in it. When Bhai died, she was reduced to a cipher as a person.

~

So we packed our belongings and came back to Saat Rasta. There was tension between us, and Aai added to it. In the beginning, Namdeo behaved well with Aai. But he was not in the habit of offering respect to someone older than him. And he was drinking.

~

It was Ashu's birthday. Neither of us wanted to make a big thing out of it. We didn't even celebrate Diwali but we made an exception for Ashu's birthday and had lights, garlands et cetera. We decided that everyone should have a biryani meal. Two hundred people were to be cooked for but we weren't going to have any help in, oh no, just a chef from the Taj Mahal Hotel.

I don't know what manner of chef he was; I could have cooked better than that. The food was terrible. I had never heard of such an odd menu either: just biryani and kadhi. And just before the birthday, a terrible ruckus.

One of the party workers had an idea: on Ashu's birthday, an image of the Buddha must be installed and everyone should pray before it. Namdeo agreed immediately. I was furious. 'No one is going to pray in this house,' I said, Namdeo got angry. So did his father. I had read a little about Buddhist beliefs and philosophy. The ideas were, of course, sublime. But on certain matters, they were clear. Do not create idols, the Buddha had said. Do not worship them. I am not a prophet. Do not follow what I say simply because I say it. Become your own pathfinder. Become your own torch-bearer. And so I told them what I had read. But such was their misfortune that though they had accepted this belief system, they had, in Buddha's own land, turned him into a God. They prayed to him, they garlanded his statues, they lit candles, they bowed down in worship. I was totally against such blind belief. The fight went on and on until two in the morning. Namdeo said that if the birthday were to be celebrated at all, Buddhist prayers would have to be part of it. I retorted: 'These things will not do in this house. I have protected my child from blind faith and I will not teach him to believe without reason.' I refused to back down. So what if we did not celebrate? That wasn't going to stop him from growing up. Finally, Namdeo gave in. The party worker, whose bright idea this had been, sulked for a while and then left the next day without eating.

~

As soon as I got to Mumbai, I began to look for a job. I searched for a long time until Dadasaheb Rupwate[54] got me a job in eight days. Film City…the first step of my dream ladder. Some distance away from Goregaon, in the Aarey Milk Colony area, a huge piece of land had been turned into a government-run film studio and other amenities such as a laboratory and recording rooms had been set up. There were gardens, lakes and a helipad. Around it, a hill, water bodies, and dense green forests. Everything that a filmmaker would need to make a film was to be found here and it was all out in the open, in a natural setting, my favourite surroundings.

Added to that the actors and actresses, the shootings. I had a clerical post in the office. There was not much work in the first few months but I was terribly happy with my job. The glamorous faces of the film stars, their style, their behaviour, the pleasant peaceful atmosphere. It was also at this time that I started a music class but I could not concentrate. It was all too rushed. I had to get from the job at Goregaon to the music class at Dadar

---

[54]Dadasaheb Damodar Tatyaba Rupwate (1928-1999) was the first rector of Siddharth College of Arts, Science and Commerce. He was an Ambedkarite and after Dr Babasaheb Ambedkar's death, editor of *Prabuddha Bharata*. In 1948, he set up the Bahujan Shikshan Samaj and was often a member of the Maharashtra cabinet of ministers with portfolios that included social welfare housing and culture.

Hindu Colony and then back home and straight into the kitchen. I was exhausted. My salary was three hundred and fifty rupees but that would be gone in two days and I was writing nothing.

Namdeo was drinking and brawling as always. Sometimes the boozing would go on all night. And, of course, he could not be doing this quietly. There would always be a bunch of loafers from Kamathipura: hoodlums and toughs, workers, friends, and they would talk about the Panthers, they would abuse and debate and recite poetry—in all this, how could I practise music? And then there were the fights that never seemed to end...

During the time I was looking for a job I took admission in the Shreemati Nathibai Damodar Thackersey (SNDT) University. I wanted very badly to study. My sixth subject was singing. Then I got a job. Right up to the preliminary examinations, I attended college regularly. When I got the job, I became an external student. The music class I took outside was like extra tuition in the sixth subject. Cooking, working, the singing class, studying and writing, it was all very strenuous.

The fights would leave me disturbed. I had sought a new direction from my life. I stopped cooking. From my earnings I would buy anda pao. I had broken off all ties with Namdeo. There was no conversation between us. I began to secrete away a few vessels and books on my side of the partition. Then one day I got a door put into the partition and locked it and cut him off entirely. I was on one side, he on the other. When I was at home, Ashu was always with me. He slept by my side. As he had always felt the heat very much, even as a child, he did not fall asleep easily. I had to fan him until he fell asleep. The fan was on the other side of the partition, you see. From that side, Namdeo would taunt me and hurl abuse.

Sometimes he would call softly, affectionately. Sometimes he would come to eat. Or he would bring me something to eat and call me over. I would not go.

The exams were close. The fights and the mental tension kept my head buzzing. I had been studying. Since all the subjects were things I loved, I only had to read the material once for it to go into my head. But I could not find any interest in singing. And the first paper was singing. I only knew the ten major ragas by heart; that was all. I knew nothing of the taals. I couldn't tell an ektaal from a tritaal and a jhaptaal. And armed with those ten ragas, I set foot in the examination hall. I picked up the tanpura with a trace of nervousness. The examiners gave me a raga to sing. I plucked a string, hummed a note or two and suddenly came to a grinding halt. That was the wrong note, the wrong chord. The examiners gave me some time and then suggested a second raga. I pulled myself together and tried to find the note but nothing came back. I had forgotten everything. My head was a blank. What was going on? The raga, the alaap, the aaroh, the avaaroh...where had they all gone?

The examiners saw my state.

'Sing any raga you know,' onc said sternly.

I could not raise my eyes. My blood was poison in my veins. I wanted Mother Earth to open up and take me back into her womb. I wanted to die right there. What had happened? Why could I not remember a single note? Defeated, I went home and since that day I never tried to learn music. Before this, I had put my name down for seven or eight singing classes but something always went wrong. Either the house would be in an uproar or I would have a sinus attack or our home would be taken from us. On three separate occasions, I registered for a dance class, a typing class and a telephone operator's course. I joined a dance group. And after a few days, just when I thought I might be able to do this, my mind would collapse in fatigue. I would not be able to manage. It would all seem meaningless. I went to so many places and met so many people and tried to learn so many things and failed each time.

My voice is still a good one, even today. I hum to myself sometimes. I think Namdeo fell in love with my voice.

Even so, after our marriage, he did not support me in anything I tried. On the contrary, when I picked up my tanpura for riyaaz, he would mock my efforts. When I sang, he would shout, 'Shut up.' This was life-threatening in a way. I felt sick of my life. Was this the same man who had played a tape recording of my singing up to two and three in the morning? For here he was, trying his best to silence me.

After that, he went to Nasik for a while. He drank a lot and brawled and brangled to his heart's content. Some people got together and gave him a sound thrashing. That night, someone threw him into a taxi and dumped him on our doorstep. They had made a thorough job of it. His whole body was swollen, his face black and blue. In the morning, Aai woke me up to tell me.

Angrily I said, 'Forget it, Aai. Let him die.'

He heard this and got angry. I refused to go and see him. Aai was truly frightened of him. And this angered me too. We had severe fights and I could see that these tormented both of us but I never stopped hurting him. I wanted to take revenge on him, revenge for all that he had done. On my way out, I looked at him and without even being aware of it, I gasped in sympathy. This irritated him further and so I left for work.

He was not paying rent. Nor would he help with the electricity bill. Aai would often mention this. Since he now had a fever, he would leave the light on all night. Aai told him to switch it off. I added my two cents' worth. He got up in the morning and hit me, hit me hard.

Furious, I told him he should leave.

In a few days he did leave. The house was empty for he dragged Ashu away too.

Despite my job, I began to write again. A lot. Some poems, essays, plays…all scattered now.

I went to see Niloufer,[55] a famous lawyer with Leftist sympathies. She agreed to take my case.

The job was going well. The atmosphere was as I might wish it, with good officers who understood my situation. I wanted to write but I could not. In the world, the clerical community is very narrow-minded and funny. I did not fit in with them and this made some of them very angry. But most people were quite kind and affectionate. Sometimes I would have to take leave because of the fights in the house and this would annoy some of my fellow-workers. But something started cooking in my mind. I would go to Film City and watch the shootings. The actors, the directors, the stars, from Hema Malini to Amitabh and Rekha, and the stories about them. The humiliating lives of the extras. This was my field of endeavour and I had to be detached from it. My dream was to hand but I could not reach out and grab it. I knew many people in the industry but I was very shy. All this was unbearable. I found myself in the same rut again.

~

[55]Niloufer Bhagwat is a famous lawyer who worked with the Committee for the Protection of Democratic Rights. She is the wife of the former chief of the Indian Navy, Vishnu Bhagwat.

During the year of the court case, I would often miss the dates of the hearing. And so one day, Niloufer told me: 'The courts won't come and camp on your doorstep. Suppose the judge passes an order and you're missing and he simply walks off with the child, what then?'

I had to think this through. For the last seven to eight months, I had been fighting for my rights to the child. Each Saturday and every second and fourth Friday,[56] I would catch the train at Goregaon and get off at Andheri and take a bus to his home, or rather to Latif-bhaiyya's flat. Then I would take Ashu and catch the train to Saat Rasta again. Ashu would spend the weekend with me. The house would fill up with his chirping. We would go out and wander the city: to the Jehangir Art Gallery and to the beach. In the night, his Bespectacled Granny would tell him stories. And on Monday, Namdeo would come to collect him again.

Ashu's world revolved around me but what could he do? That we were playing with his young life disturbed me greatly.

Once when I went to Andheri, Namdeo took hold of my arm and would not let go. It was not possible for me to think of staying there. Ashu's face filled with sorrow. His eyes showed me that he wanted me to be there.

---

[56]This refers to the government of Maharashtra's work timings. Second and fourth Saturdays are holidays. The other Saturdays are working days.

Arré deva. What was I to do?

I begged Namdeo: 'Let me take him today. You can fetch him later.'

He refused. He wanted to trap me. I would stay, he believed, if only for the child's sake.

If a man could be reduced to ash with a glance, Namdeo would have been incinerated that evening. But he was adamant. I put a stone on my heart and I left although a thousand voices were screaming inside me. I despised Namdeo with every drop of my blood. He was playing with me. He had snatched away my child and I could do nothing confronted with his patriarchal prerogative. All the way home, I wept.

~

I could not conceive of a life in which I chose my own happiness over the well-being of my child. Namdeo would often come home. He would often ask permission to return.

I was very angry. I wanted revenge. He claimed to love his son beyond all things but he could cruelly separate that same son from his mother when he could see the child's unhappiness writ large on his small face. Once when he came to Saat Rasta to take Ashu, something snapped inside me.

In a savage voice, I said: 'You cannot have the child. You have no rights over him.'

'What are you saying?'

'He isn't yours in the first place.'

The man with him and my mother were both shocked but the attack failed. Namdeo was peaceable. He only smiled a little.

'Makes no difference. Now he's mine. He's in my control. And I love him with my life. Don't they sometimes exchange children in the hospital? I'll take it that something like that happened.'

I was annoyed. I told Niloufer what had happened.

'I'll claim he isn't the father. Then I'll get my child back, won't I?'

She looked at me for a couple of moments in surprise.

'Is that what you're planning to say?'

'Yes. I will get the child, won't I?'

She couldn't guarantee it. But she had showed that she was ready to help and that was a big thing.

I had been fighting so long and I had been fighting alone. I was making a laughing stock of myself. I was also laughing at myself. And weeping for myself. Facing my loneliness, facing the bitter truth every night, embracing this truth as I fell asleep.

Peace of mind? What kind of animal is that?

~

Defeated, I returned to Andheri. Namdeo came to fetch me. I was no abhsarika, stealing away under cover of night to meet her secret lover; nor was I the wife of the leader Namdeo Dhasal. I was only Ashu's mother.

The Andheri flat was in a middle-class area. Behind the closed doors of their flats, people seemed to be imprisoned. Here all my relationships were broken. I had no friends, no relatives, no confidantes, no one. At 9 or 10 p.m., I would walk alone through those empty and deserted streets, my mind in a storm. How was I to break out of this prison? The habit of loneliness is difficult to form so I formed others. I began to drink beer. I began to smoke cigarettes. I neglected my diet and drank tea instead. All day tea; at night, beer. I had subconsciously decided to destroy myself.

After Ashu, I had become pregnant three times but Namdeo's infidelities and his snatching away of Ashu had poisoned me so thoroughly that I did not want to bear any more of his children. The insults he had offered to me as a mother would be impossible to forget for the rest of my life.

Birth-control pills did not agree with me. Namdeo refused to use any prophylactics. His attitude was: what happens, happens. He had no thought for my mental devastation, my physical weakness. I refused to carry his child in my body. And then it seemed as if my very body would reject the foetuses. In the garden next to the house grew some papaya trees. If I was late, I would go and eat raw papayas and cashews, drink beer. The papaya would leave my lips sore and ulcers would develop.

Then a doctor, a visit to Pearl Centre,[57] and in the first month I would free myself and return. I would go alone. He did not have the consideration or sensitivity to come with me or to send anyone with me. Later, I had an operation on my nose. I have always had trouble with my sinuses but this man did not have the forethought or the kindness to offer me my bus fare to the hospital, let alone the cab fare. What had happened to his love? Where was his humanity?

~

Namdeo would come home drunk. I would refuse, on these occasions, to sleep with him. I did not want children and certainly not with this man. He would insist, physically forcing me to come near him. I would say, 'Be right back' and go into the bathroom, bolt the door and stand there for an hour, sometimes two. If he had drunk enough, he would go off to sleep. Then I would creep out on little cat's feet and drop down next to Ashu.

That year in Andheri went very badly. I did not mind the economic instability but I could not bear the thought of spending the rest of my life fighting and weeping. Was I to be lonely for the rest of my life?

Namdeo would mock what he called my middle-class behaviour.

---

[57]Pearl Centre, Dadar-Parel, is a well-known abortion clinic.

'There's no humanity in you. No food to give others. Not even tea. Instead of just serving it, you ask, "Will you have tea?" as a Brahmin would. What kind of humanity is that?'

But the same Namdeo would never show me the humanity he claimed to have in such full measure.

This happened when I went to Kolhapur. Aai had gone to Andheri to visit but his mother and father locked the door on her and kept her on the doorstep. So much for their humanity. When I heard this my blood began to boil. I was angry but this time it was the venomous anger of a female cobra.

'If I do not make your parents sit on my mother's doorstep, I will never use my own name again.' I promised myself.

I kept my word.

~

Later I heard another story. After I got married, the poet who had been enamoured of me, swallowed some Diazone pills and tried to kill himself. He was very ill after that. Even today, I find it difficult to meet his eyes. I remember reading a wise saying somewhere: 'Don't marry the man you love. Marry a man who loves you.'

Anyway, marriage is a gamble.

~

After those abortions, I grew emaciated. I was changing inside. My heart was hardening too. I was gaining strength from that which did not kill me. I was becoming bitter. I began to feel nothing. And I started fighting back.

I decided that there was not much point to mewling away in a corner. If I wanted happiness, I would have to snatch at it. I would have to take it from the world. My own life taught me this rare and valuable lesson. Now my life had turned into a challenging game. I accepted the dare. The gauntlet was thrown down: by one man, by every man, by my circumstances.

I picked it up.

9

Namdeo developed pleurisy. He was treated of course, but he was proud of his illness. Whenever he fell ill, he would be very pleased with himself. For he could not be suffering from something ordinary; he was always sure he had developed jaundice or leprosy or cancer. Having diagnosed himself, he would rush off for medical assistance. The doctors were well aware of this. I found it all irresistibly funny. I would say, 'Don't give them so much trouble. Or you might read headlines in the paper tomorrow: "Tired of examining hypochondriac, doctor commits suicide"'. And my laughter would bubble over.

When he had been beaten up at Nashik and brought home, I was on my side of the partition. From there,

I could hear him telling and retelling his exploits to whoever came to see him.

'And then, you know, ten people came at me. Can you imagine? Anyone else would have run away but not me. Oh no. I wasn't less. I gave as good as I got.'

The next visitor would hear the same record.

'And can you imagine, twenty to twenty-five people coming at me with sticks…'

As days passed and as visitors arrived, the numbers increased. From twenty-five, it went to fifty and from there to hundred and soon it was two hundred men.

I would laugh until the tears ran down my face.

'What lies you tell! Even your tall tales should be reasonable. If two hundred men had attacked you, would we even have found your bones?'

I was very outspoken then. This truly annoyed him. My poetry collection was published by Namdeo and we fought again. Narayan Athavale left the press. A court order impounded the press. My book would have sold as waste paper but one of the workers informed me of what was about to happen. I gave him some money to bring me the half-printed books. I sent these to Continental in Pune and got them printed. Aai put in two thousand rupees of her own money. The rest was Namdeo's money. In the end I acknowledged my gratitude to Namdeo. There was no way to sell it to bookshops so I just distributed copies.

Namdeo would get new ideas all the time. Since these were never planned properly, they failed. I would tell him: 'If I were in your place, I would now have bungalows in the major metros and produced films of my own.'

But he could never be pragmatic and turn his ideas into reality. Namdeo's friends had an unspoken right over everything he bought. They would come and take his things away. I stopped bothering about this, stopped even mentioning it. Manohar Ankush, a revolutionary leader, came to stay. When he was leaving, he stole Namdeo's money and later even sent him a letter saying, 'What did you need the money for? You have everything,' and that kind of nonsense. This made me angry. When we did not have money, my ornaments went to the pawnshop, I went out selling the magazines as waste paper. That was how we had survived. And these were now the people we encountered?

~

Once, one of his relatives came over. He was a frequent visitor.

We had dinner. The three of us were at home: Namdeo, he and I. And what does he do? He asks for me.

'Let's have some fun. Come into the other room. Let's make Namdeo jealous.'

I was stunned. To me women's liberation did not mean sleeping around. I refused. And so he turned to Namdeo.

'Come on, why don't you persuade her?'

Namdeo looked at my face for a moment and said, 'I'm not going to tell her anything. If she wants to sleep with you, she will come herself.'

I got angry with Namdeo. But the man never came again.

~

What was true? What was real? The twisted and poisoned society around me? The women who bore rape and abuse at the hands of their husbands while concealing the evidence of being brutalized? The buying and selling of ideals in the political marketplace? The leaders who wore the badge of revolution to cover their price tags? The artists who wanted to live off their art but were ignored and eked out a half-starved life? Or was reality the outsider I had become? Was my incomplete, neglected existence a reality? Was my personal sorrow to be my jail? What could I do for myself? And what could I do for those around me?

I watched the Dalit movement blaze across the sky but I also watched it crash and burn as it sold itself cheap. I had seen it breaking up. I became a part of it but I was still detached from it. Is it a mistake to talk about this? Is it right to criticize a movement that has just been born? But what had happened was also true, was it not? Doubt, despair and disbelief were in every eye. Our circumstances do not change with the change in the ruling party. No party, no organization, no leader, no minister seems to be able to make this change. Having understood this truth, I am conscious every moment of their indifference.

Many a goonda turned up at the door. Pistols against their chests, knives tied to their ankles. They had cold brutal cruel eyes. They had powerful sinewy bodies. They brought with them the implicit threat that violence could explode at any moment. They were residents of Kamathipura and they fought, sometimes among themselves, sometimes with others, but they fought all the time. They were so care-a-damn you felt that at any moment, they'd wrap up the world and throw it on the rubbish heap. I watched all this and I saw their anger dissipated and their courage wasted. Their anger, their unhappiness, their discontent, their anarchic rage, their strength of body, all wasted.

Namdeo turned them all into Panthers, man-eating jaguars. He had helped many of them. They offered him respect. They used him too. Namdeo chose to forget all this or to ignore it. He would say, 'The lumpen class is like that. They have no role to play. Working them is difficult but it will change slowly.'

Namdeo was an incurable optimist. A dyed-in-the-wool organizer. He would fall a thousand times, he would bash his head a thousand times against a wall, but he would get up again and go back for more. Only to build up his organization.

I had no interest in all this. Today, I don't even find much to read in Marathi poetry. I get bored of it. There does not seem to be much creativity left. My reading has been reduced to nothing. I am myself wandering aimlessly.

Not one tree remains to protect
The nest of my dreams.
How many years have passed?
The silks of my youth have been
Scooped up in my lover's beak
And he has flown away.

I read a book about Vincent Van Gogh and was stunned by it. Can anyone live a life like that? To such an extreme level of self-destruction. To be so passionate about something. To be intoxicated by ideas. To live illuminated by the burning intensity of the sun.

What stayed with me was the Van Gogh who could cut off his ear and send it as a gift to his beloved; the Van Gogh who could paint in the heat of the sun until his skin burned so he could capture the colour of the sunlight.

There is a line in that book: 'I never try to free myself from sorrow because very often it is sorrow that allows an artist to express himself with all his power.'

That I could understand completely. What a man

this was. I had been living the life of a cockroach. Chee. When one feels revulsion for the self, there is nothing so shaming in the world. The fact that I had not been able to do anything new must mean that my life is worthless. I seemed to spend my days in a whirlwind with questions and issues hurled about, as I sought answers to the discontent that is within me. Why could I not simply transcend one man?

It is true that defeat teaches you many valuable lessons. Of these, the most important one is that it teaches you to recognize who you are, your faults, your limitations, your strengths.

To accept defeat is almost as painful an experience as the defeat itself. To see oneself falling into an abyss and to be aware that one cannot save oneself is terrifying.

But one thing did happen. I had been totally devoid of self-confidence. But this defeat made me rich, rich in experience and rich in confidence. This was an extraordinary change that began to take place in me. I grew tired of despair and became aggressive and tough. I became hot-tempered and obstinate but tenacious in pursuit of an idea. I turned into a rebel. I would not bear even a slighting word or two. I would respond in kind, sharply, and take the blows that followed. Through the pain, I would continue to make suitable reply. I peeled off the layers of deceit and falsity and hypocrisy from the self as one might peel a banana. My real femininity was now primitive, unashamed, intense, aggressive; but also sensitive.

My understanding of the world was hard-won, paid for in blows. I began to become aware of the change in my personality. But I could not stop it either. It troubled me for I had loved the feminine side to my nature, that earlier version of me.

Why did I find it impossible to break this umbilicus? Why did I find it difficult to live an innocent, harmless life? I could not live within the framework of convention nor could I challenge the ones in which I now found myself. I felt half-baked, incomplete, and this stymied my own attempts at self-exploration. Something had to burst inside.

Nothing happened.

I have always loved nature. At ten or eleven in the night, I would go to the sea and sit there alone. This was a source of great joy to me. The entire city would be asleep and exhausted but I would be awake and alone. I had wandered the city at night, in taxis and on foot. I had walked around the city at night with Namdeo so often.

~

Malabar Hill and the road that snaked up it, shining and sleepy and empty, the surrounding darkness like a piece of bevelled glass; the ink-dark sea, the lights of the city like a gemstone-heavy garland, their shivering reflections in the mirror of the ocean…the city by night is unequalled. It is quiet, silent. It is a drug, an addiction that soaks your entire body. The sound of the sea is solemn and composed. One's life becomes small in the presence of this expansive corner of the world. It is as if silence has spread through space like a blank canvas. I feel I have immersed myself in the sharp but tolerant soul of the city. The deep solemn roar of the sea dissolves me. Nothing remains. I am no one. And then suddenly I feel a deep yearning. A formless, limitless void. A sea that you can barely see in the dark but of which you are aware at the level of the breath. And the land that holds the roots of my life and my being. It is a reassuring touch, those pebbles even. The wisps of gentle breeze. I am part of all this, this wordless, happy, huge truth. I want to dissolve into it.

Why should my life be a sacrifice to one man? I am a woman, a force of nature. I am a symbol of all this, this overarching, overwhelming, bliss-soaked nature.

I rise, casting off the old, a snake that has moulted. That pull, that experience rasps across my body.

~

At this time Kamathipura is beginning to come alive. At every window and at every door hang garlands of flesh. Everywhere, swaying animals of the two-footed variety. Their gaze sweeps across you, a live thing, an animal that is licking its lips, drooling. I remember a line from one of my stories:

'If a part of your body rots, you can at least cut it off and throw it away. But this city, this alley...you can't cut it away, you can't throw it away, you can't escape it.'

Two different worlds. Two different worlds which come together for a moment and without ever making contact, drift apart again, leaving me disturbed.

I did not want to be stamped 'Romantic'. But that is exactly what my nature is. This realization made me uncomfortable.

I watched Kamathipura, safely, from behind the rolled-up glass of a taxi window. The road was one I had travelled so often it was a habit. When I was working with a women's group, I had often asked for donations. Many women thought this odd. But the Nepali women drove me away. I tried, despite this, to get close to them. But their contempt was clear in their white faces, as if they knew we were different and that I would never be able to enter their world.

When I turned to go home, I felt like an old woman. I was burdened with an impotent anger. In despair, I dug my teeth into my wrist.

This restlessness, this sense of being incomplete, when will I be able to put a full-stop to it? I am middle class. I love with abandon. These are my faults. My political knowledge is inadequate. I have never even wanted to acquire a deeper and fuller understanding of it. Because, today, values and commitments seem like a joke to everyone. Those who truly want to do something end up devastated or sell their souls for power and money. In this country, political people are only of two kinds: the sold-out and the bombed-out. Very few others find any other way out.

I had known some of the Communist Party of India members since childhood. They too drew away because of Namdeo's politics and his crude behaviour. I still feel close to the Communists and their ideologies. But if you're creative, I believe, you should not be committed to any party.

Whatever I may have felt about Namdeo's selling out, whatever I may have felt about his political beliefs and private behaviour, however much I may have distanced myself from them, I knew that to the world, I was Namdeo's wife and it was assumed that I was in agreement with what he did. I hated this. No one seemed willing to recognize that a wife is also a woman who might have an independent existence and her own beliefs.

Even if there has been some change in the way caste is treated in our city, our mental make-up remains unchanged. I do not think that conversion has brought much change in Dalit society. They have replaced statues of Mari-aai and Yellamma with images of the Buddha. That seems to be all. I, at least, don't know of any political movement that can cut across the caste system. All political parties, of course, emphatically claim to be inclusive.

That the Communist leadership was largely Brahmin and that Dr Babasaheb Ambedkar had not allowed the Communists too close meant that the Dalits did not allow the Communists to work among them. The Naxalite movement is underground. They are staunch in their romantic rebellion. The Dalit movement is a complete mess. Everyone is doing 'something or the other'. Of course, what passion, if any, informs their actions, is anyone's guess. The politics of the ruling class has no relationship to the lives of the common people. There are dozens of groups, each with its own mahatma. And yet in every eye, there is a burgeoning tree of despair, its roots spreading like an octopus.

~

To write an account as I have is supposed to be an act of shamelessness.

But I believe that the suffering I have experienced and the experiences I have undergone are common to women all over the city and even in the villages. Women everywhere live lives like mine but their sensibilities have been blunted. Perhaps it is a curse to have a sensitive mind.

Like Gandhari, the middle-class woman chooses a golden blindfold. It is respectable to do this but it is also mad and foolish. Men are moved when they watch the sufferings of women, the physical or mental rape that is depicted in arthouse movies. But don't they knowingly or unknowingly do exactly the same thing?

Basically men, all men, constitute a single species. There are no differences of caste or creed among them. They have no culture. I do not say women have culture either. The whole concept of Bharatiya sanskriti or Indian culture is, according to me, a laughable dead animal. Everyone flogs this poor dead horse and takes a piece of its hide to cover up something they want to do. But underneath this thin disguise, the grim face of the violent male animal can be discerned. This is the naked muddy messy truth. For a piece of bread, a beggar will fight a dog. Another may look on, in a detached way, and then hurry off to catch a train. To be able to see pain and ignore it is part of our culture.

Ninety-five per cent of women who say, 'My married life is going rather well,' are telling lies. At least those who feel the need to express their own identity and those who are aware of the need for self-expression. But every woman should be proud of herself and her individuality and should be able to express those needs.

From the city to the village, from the penthouse suite to the slum, every woman stands on the same ground. She is benumbed, confused, and she endures. If you believe that the world is full of predatory males, that they may never be evaded or eluded, you dare not risk demonstrating a self. So you obliterate it in order to survive.

In all the rush and push of the political struggle, the question of women's rights will never be addressed. I know this all too well. For every politician addresses every question only after he makes sure his own rights have been secured. In other words, most progressive men (!) believe that it is up to women to do 'something or the other' to empower other women and further the struggle for women's rights. And this while women are not allowed to leave the house to help other women. Men cannot get beyond women's bodies. These are the two failures of the movement.

The male ego is the most dangerous and twisted thing in our society. And serving this ego is supposed to be the highest goal of a woman's life. This seems to be the same thing as the tree in the fable that gives its branch to make an axe for the woodcutter.

My life cannot be made over to anyone, not even Namdeo Dhasal.

Men and women are two aspects of humanity, equal to each other. Both are incomplete without the other but strong in themselves. A woman has an independent brain and the ability to think. Why should she accept the superiority of man, suppressing herself?

'Behind every successful man stands a woman,' they say. I want to erase this saying entirely.

Some Memories

Suddenly some memories prick me sharply, like thorns in a cactus. Or perhaps they were buried and have been unearthed.

Pain was like the burning orb of the sun that hovered on the horizon of my existence. I could refuse nothing. I could not run away. I was being dragged along and this was against my very nature.

In the life of a political man, this kind of dragging is natural, even inevitable. He becomes wise after taking some jolts and shocks and tries to make as many compromises as necessary in order to live securely. This is my understanding of it. But it might be argued that he had brought this tumult upon himself and so perhaps it fits in with his ideological principals and he tries to bear with the consequences. But what of those with him, the workers, the wife? What is their role in all this?

Namdeo's workers had accepted him as their leader unconditionally. So they did not feel there was much difference between him and the movement. They simply needed a peg on which to hang their faith and he was that peg.

But what about me? Why should I be dragged along? I had not accepted any of Namdeo's aims, nor his strategies nor the decisions he took nor his slippery ideologies. I did not understand politics well but this did not mean that I could stumble down a road labelled 'Sell-Out'. For example, he tied up with the Shiv Sena and I did not approve at all.

'What have you to do with it? What do you know?' With these two sentences, he would dismiss my protests.

But then what had I to do with it? And what did I know? He was responsible, yes, but still I have to ask: Was I the only one to create the fights?

He brought home lots of money. From where? I did not know. And it was not as if he was going to tell me, were I to ask. Ashu got whatever he asked for as well as things he did not ask for. But Namdeo always spent more money on his organization than on his home. There were ten to fifteen thousand posters to be printed and then the workers who stuck them up had to be paid. They got liquor and money for everything, from their clothes to their shoes and the cash with which they paid the prostitutes of Kamathipura Lane No 1. His political life was already a mess but his love for his workers and his organization was beyond question. If there were no money for a political programme, our tape recorder, my ornaments, would all end up with the Marwadi. When it came to that, he would beg money from friends or cheat these hoods. I hated this because I had been brought up to believe that one should not owe the grocer or anyone else but he owed everyone and I was caught in the trap of his indebtedness. 'These things happen in a movement,' he would say. His love for his workers was similarly demonic. They would be abused often and roundly. When he was very angry, he would even slap them. Whatever came to hand—shoes, sticks—could be used and was used to his heart's content. But the strange thing was that a few minutes later, this rage would abate and they would all be arm in arm, chatting chummily and going off together.

I could never understand how this bond of blood, of caste, could be so tough and enduring. 'He's from my caste,' was all it took. This one phrase was enough for a man's behaviour to change. I have never experienced either the security or the benefits of such blood and caste relationships but then I do not accept these as valid.

If a man makes a mistake, it is accepted that he must be forgiven by his caste members or family; and more than that, his actions must be justified and rationalized. Those who forgive Namdeo's 'mistakes' on the basis of being of the same caste as he, are, in my eyes, as guilty as Namdeo. If a poet, however great, commits murder, would society forgive him?

Everyone seems to feel that if they are doing social work, they are doing society a great big favour. They do not see it as a duty, a contribution they must make. Making speeches about human rights is all very well. They would never test them in everyday life. I am not singling out one caste or religious group here. It is the same everywhere.

~

Even after all this, I am still filled with a lust for life.

'It is a good thing my Lord that I am bankrupt,' sang Sant Tukaram. I cannot be philosophical about it as he was. There are moments when I want to become an ascetic but that is just a spasm and passes soon. Many people have told me, 'Write in a detached way.' But we tend to love ourselves too much for that. To place oneself at a distance from the self and observe one's life is difficult. I have been wounded so badly and so often that if I think back and dig deep, I sink into a morass.

For the first two years, I had to bear with society's criticism because mine had been a love marriage. This meant that I could not show my defeat to anyone; but when his behaviour hurt me, when it defeated me and left me helpless, when he deceived me, I had to deal with it on my own.

It seems to be part of man's nature to be attracted to other women. What is one to make of this? There were men hovering around me too. But because of the pressures of society and tradition, I kept the faith with Namdeo. I do not make commitments lightly.

After three or four years of torture, I decided to overthrow those inhibitions, to do away with my shyness and sacrifices. I had not slept well in years. There was a poisonous reality standing in the middle of my life with its arms stretched out.

And I was being scorched by it.

My people did not keep in touch with Namdeo. They were avoiding us. It was not a question of caste; it was a question of his attitude. His foul mouth meant that people avoided him for he could say anything in front of anyone and in the most foul and abusive language. People did not take issue with him about it. But it made me explode inside and it made life intolerable.

When I returned after leaving him for six or seven months, Ashu had learned to abuse. The party workers and his father found this amusing and even admirable. I had to break the habit with a combination of scolding and beating.

Namdeo's late-coming made me very angry. I hated waiting for him, especially in the night. Waiting for anyone is a hateful business. It shames the person who waits.

I would wait, wondering where he had gone, what he was doing. And the memories of old hurts would return to plague me until he arrived. Slowly the night would advance upon me, red in tooth and claw. This endless waiting would seem like the night had driven needles into my eyes. I would feel a great rage that he was cheating me. I had been clean and open. He had entered and despoiled every area of my life. I would tell him all my thoughts and feelings. When we were together, I had told him everything I felt, without holding anything back, the naughty and the nice, it had all come out. I held nothing close to my chest. And yet he thought nothing of lying to me? He felt nothing about his assuaging his desires in brothels as any lecher might? All those fine words and fine thoughts—what right did people like this have to make fine speeches?

Man? What manner of beast is he? What tree does he come from? What are the criteria for masculinity? Many laws and terms can be defined but who can define what it means to be a man? Hitting a woman is also a matter of masculinity. Fathering a son is also about masculinity. Producing sterile and negative literature is also a matter of masculinity.

My ideal husband would be debonair, smart, understanding, an aficionado of the arts. He would understand who I was, and most important, he would love only me. As a friend, he would encourage my artistic side.

This was my dream. It stayed a dream. I discovered that ideals are laughable and have no place in reality. Men do not have ideals. It seems they cannot have them. The signs of humanity are not decided on the basis of ideals.

And so I realized an unnamed desire from my childhood. I was now a heroine in a tragic novel. Sorrow would be my lifelong companion, its grip vise-like upon my wrist.

I could not abandon Ashu nor could Ashu do without me. Actually, I didn't care for children. But that isn't the reason why I avoided taking responsibility for him. What right did I have to sacrifice the life of a child so that I might find a solution to a problem of my own making?

Could I play with his life as Namdeo had played with mine? Could I resist any injustice done to me unless I, on my part, refused to do injustice to others? Childhood is one link we have with humanity.

Whether the child was mine or someone else's, I had no right to hurt it. If you cannot help a child achieve her dreams, at least you should not take those dreams away from her.

However, this is not the way of the world. Because of social disparities, the internal contradictions in people and scary reality, children become old before their time. Their childhood is taken from them.

Namdeo's organization had its base in Kamathipura from the very beginning. His 'beautiful' childhood had been spent there. So he would always return there.

However you imagine 'Hell', however you define 'Hell', all of it is here. Thin and irritable children, men whose eyes strip the clothes off your body, all locked in an incessant all-day, all-night battle. There was an unending stream of people who came and went. There were fights, knives, acid bulbs, pistols, chains, tube-lights and from the restaurants, a steady supply of soda-water bottles. All these things were owned by one of the gangsters of the area.

At one or two in the night, a taxi would stop in front of the house. The bolt would be rattled loudly, harshly, shaking me out of my sleep. One of them would be at the door with 'Dada, come quick.'

Or perhaps, 'The fight's on. That Such-and-Such beat up So-and-So.'

Or else, 'Butter Vilas was beaten up by those party guys. Come on, quick. They hit him on the head with a sword and it came right out of his stomach. Oof, the blood.'

The speakers were always tight. I would be only half-awake, sleep still clouding my eyes. I would be angry but I still could not resist asking who this mighty man of valour might be who could drive his sword through someone's head and bring it out of his stomach.

Namdeo would go off immediately. Sometimes he would be in the mood for love. If that midnight knock came in the middle of our lovemaking, he would forget about me and get up and go. For one's husband to rise from one's side and go is a painful experience. I would mutter and mumble in a rage. Sleep would not return. One a.m. 2 a.m. Three. Four. Five. The sound of a tap. A cock crowing. Half-awake in this off-key world, alone, insecure and in this perpetual state of waiting, I would hear the taxi a long way off. I'd get up and open the door. Then the usual annoyance, complaints, sulks, silences, explanations, persuasions. Sometimes, we would have a fight and I would abuse the party workers but Namdeo could never understand or empathize with my emotional state during those nights.

~

Namdeo received a great deal of love from people, more love than he could digest. Too much happiness can also hurt. Truly he was the lover made of sand, always slipping through your fingers; the sand-man who would not allow any stamp to be set upon him.

~

I almost forgot. In the first year of our marriage, Namdeo had visited a prostitute and contracted a venereal disease. I had no idea about this. He would take me everywhere he went. One day we ended up in front of a clinic somewhere in Pila House. Outside there was a line of young men with faded eyes, and some older ones. Namdeo went inside. I remained standing there but when it grew warm, I followed him inside. There was not a single woman there. All the men began to look at me rather peculiarly. Angry and confused, I hurried out. And only then did I discover that it was a venereal disease clinic. I could have died of shame. I was very angry and we fought all day about this.

~

So many revolting experiences. And yet I feel eager to recount them. Why should I feel any love of life?

What a great yearning for love I had. And what a desert I found myself in.

At one point, after Namdeo had hit me, I went to make a police complaint. But the police only register your complaint. They don't do anything about it. I discovered then that they are not here to protect one or to deliver justice.

I said, 'He beat me. He threatened to kill me. I need protection.'

'You have registered your complaint, right?' And then, with an unconcerned smile, he asked me: 'So, are you planning a second marriage?'

I felt like hitting him but I also wanted to hit myself for having come to the wrong place. This is the ugly face of patriarchal culture. How could this filthy impotent system ensure justice for me?

~

While we were living in Bandra, Namdeo was in jail on a case someone had filed about a speech he had made. I was completely broke. No provisions. No kerosene, no tea, no sugar, no milk and not a paisa to buy anything. And then a couple came from Amravati to meet Namdeo and settled down to stay. I was caught in an odd situation. I explained my plight to a party worker who lived close by. He invited them to stay at his home but they wouldn't budge. Finally, I had to reveal my straitened financial circumstances to them as I had no other way out. They immediately took out some money and gave it to me.

'Bhabhi, what is there to be ashamed of in this? We are your own people. These things happen in movements like ours. Please don't worry. We'll stay here with you until Namdeo returns,' they said.

And I went out again to try and find bail for Namdeo.

The two of them were hard-core Naxalites. The Emergency tore them apart. Then the two streams parted and people were lost to each other. After that, four or five years later, I saw her in a local train. She was quite far away. I was shocked. She seemed lost; her face, emotionless and colourless. She looked at me for just a second. There was no sign of recognition on her face. Was it her?

They had lived with us for fifteen or twenty days. They had a real connection, a good relationship. They did not have children. I suspect this was out of choice as having a child can only be a hindrance to a woman in the movement.

After I saw her again, I did ask after them. My informant said: 'Didn't you hear? She went mad. A nervous breakdown. Both of them were victimized during the Emergency. Political frustration and the torture they went through broke them. And then there was the sadness of not having a child.'

That shook me. A woman seems unable to forget her own potential for motherhood. She will do injustice to her femininity but not to her maternal potential. I would see women craving motherhood.

Their strong desire for a child, for a home, shocked me. A passion for anything leads to commitment and in order to feel ready for commitment, one needs a home, a caste, a religion, a mahatma, a saint and a child.

It seems humanity looks for happiness in these bonds. Why do we believe that happiness arises only out of stability, security and commitment? It seems we are unable to rid ourselves of these archetypes. And yet isn't the desire for freedom one of the fundamental principles on which our common humanity is based? How do we forget this?

~

The days passed without meaning, as rain falls on a tin roof and runs off it. Every morning came with new people, new faces and new experiences.

When I was at Andheri, I learned to smoke cigarettes. That felt good. I thought I should try each of these potential addictions once and see what it felt like. I decided that you only live once. To live an impoverished life is also a crime. But one must also retain control of these things. I find I can content myself with a little for I formed no addictions.

I remember a line from Nietzsche. He says something to the effect that when the taste for something is at its height, it is time to stop. Those who want love perpetually understand this best.

I did not know this at all and placed a limit on everything I tried. But love was something for which I had an endless desire. I wanted more, I wanted love with commitment. I wanted someone to love me alone. Even though I knew that one could not force it.

More than one person told me. A man can do only one thing at a time. No one told me a man can love more than one at a time.

I have lived according to my ideals. Even in the times when I was starving, I would go to the pictures.

I watched Satyajit Ray's *Shatranj Ke Khiladi* alone in an empty theatre. I wept through *Sahib, Biwi aur Ghulam*, *Bandini*, and *Pyaasa*. I spent two days in a state of distress after each one. My loneliness was my only companion.

~

Compromise is such a common word but what tempests it can stir up. To live together without love is self-inflicted punishment. Many women take it for granted that they must make such compromises and accept such punishment. I can only look upon them with awe. What other feeling can one have?

I know a family, both well-educated, professors in

fact. I had gone to visit them as a child. They could not stand each other. When he entered a room, she would leave it. You could see how much the woman hated her husband. It was clearly written on her face. So, I wondered: What kept them together? What society would say? The children?

Ashu was the only bond between us. He was Namdeo's weak point while being almost totally his mother's boy. And sometimes I think: These eight years of fighting, weeping, sulking, what have they left us with? The experience?

I created nothing. Just one book of poems. That did not have much of an impact. Some people praised me but in much the same manner as one might praise a child who has just sung a song; they would metaphorically pull my cheeks and give me a chocolate.

I discovered one thing in all this. The world in general is not really interested in the experiences of the individual. What is upheld is the literature that concerns itself with social issues. The world has no time for big ideas, no time for experiences that might happen to anyone anywhere, never mind how intense the writing. This is why women's writing is not given its rightful place anywhere in the world, never mind in India. What is celebrated is the brash and the aggressive.

The experiential world of the woman is seen as circumscribed. It's not considered literature in our social sphere. Women's sensitivity is numbed; women don't study enough; women don't read enough; the questions they deal with are private and delicate. (When a monthly magazine called *Stree* was brought out for women, by women, it was assumed that only women would read it. That's where we'd find our issues and that's what we'd read.) Meena Kumari, for instance, is also treated as a woman poet. For the other canonical Urdu poets, Faiz, Maqdoom, Iqbal, et cetera, were seen as poets of the revolution who dealt with larger social questions. You won't find that in Meena Kumari's poetry. Because her writing is lyrical, sensitive and self-referential, no one takes any note of it. Her unequalled beauty and her acting talent may have also hindered an appreciation of the poet in her. Sahir Ludhianvi's 'Jinhe naaz hai Hind par woh kahaan hai?' (Where are they who have pride in India?) in Guru Dutt's film seems like a burning question. We praise Guru Dutt's aesthetic and social commitment. But his suicide is not a social issue.

This may be because today those who seek to resolve the social questions of the day do not want to clean up their own acts. They do not have the courage to ask, 'Why do we behave in the way that we behave?'

Consider a woman who has been raped. This is treated as sensational news and both politicians and journalists make capital out of it. What about the mental and psychological rape that is happening every moment? If every physical rape can be turned into political capital, who is going to bother about mental rape? Women are always the losers.

The strength of women is like the immortal endurance of Ashwatthama. I am also one of the walking wounded.

Because I could write, I have chosen to, ignoring the possibility that I will be mocked or laughed at. What do those who cannot write, do? And what can I do for them?

~

I have come through the storm. Every day there would be fifty or sixty people in the house. New faces, new introductions, new questions, new experiences.

That tomorrow would be nothing like today was the only thing that made me happy and the only thing that made me sad. It was the cause for joy and the cause for sorrow.

But it was all clearly a man's world. Every sphere belonged to them: the mehfils and the poetry readings included. I was a 'poetess'. I was made aware of my femaleness. This angered me greatly. Namdeo Dhasal's wife, was this my only identity? Why?

All the Panthers, the friends, the workers, they had fought with Namdeo at some time or the other. They would abuse him and be abused and then they'd be one again. Men seem to be better at understanding each other; perhaps they have a wider perspective, or so I felt. But when it comes to women, they have a standard scale, traditional insights and a whole system of weights and measures inside their heads. So to them, I, with my two plaits and my house dress, playing with Ashu, I was to be addressed as 'Aaho Vahini'; I was a sister-in-law, understood in terms of being the wife of their common brother. Some would show respect to your face and then talk behind your back. But none of them ever acknowledged me as a poet in my own right. And as for Namdeo it angered him that I used my father's name instead of his.

For many, our life together was a puzzle, a joke. The way we spoke freely, fought openly and kissed and made up just as openly was a marvel. But as openly as I demonstrated my love, I displayed my disgust.

My brother-in-law calls Namdeo a 'loveable rascal'. True.

When he was at work on a poem or an essay, I would often help him, summoning up in an instant the word he wanted or the synonym or the variation he was seeking. He more than anyone else acknowledged me as a talented poet.

He too is human. When he made a mistake, he was always sorry. He would apologize and almost immediately, he would make other mistakes. I loved him and hated him. Odd.

~

Who is a liberated woman? I have defined it from my own experience and in my own way.

'The woman who knows where to stop is a woman of independent mind.'

Freedom is an elastic word. It grows as much as you stretch it. If you relax the tension, it snaps back into smallness. You must insist on your freedom while still retaining your humanity.

I have found that I can always talk more freely with men than with women. Women seem to carry the burden of tradition. Men don't misconstrue things and there are no ego problems. But every man, in my experience, whether Liberal or Lohia-ite,[58] whether a follower of some ideology or a man who claims to have no ideology at all, they are all united by one belief: Every available woman is as a wife to me. This came as a terrible shock. What an innocent I was!

Namdeo said: 'I won't make any attempt but if I get a chance, I won't let it go either.'

'So why don't you leave me?' I would ask.

'Certainly not,' he would reply, 'I have one wife: Malika Amar S'eik,' and here he would maul my name a little. 'You are my only wife. But there will always be many women.'

---

[58]Refers to followers of Ram Manohar Lohia (1910-1957) who was a nationalist leader who took part in the Quit India movement.

I found this disgusting. Do women not also have our moments of attraction? But I have never gone beyond mental affairs.

~

I have opened up my heart. Suffering can make one shameless. Here you see my naked face scarred by suffering, hunger, anger and pain. We all have a streak of violence hidden in us somewhere. I have one too. It does not just display itself in complaints about my husband. Whatever side of the political spectrum one is on, humanity is beyond all ideologies. A man of high social standing should never crush a woman to attain his own ends. If you can't help, at least you should stand back.

But to turn a woman into a sacrifice to prove one's masculinity should never be acceptable in any society.

The questions, the sorrows, the experiences found in women's writing may be of no value to society. Perhaps because they don't exhibit traces of fashionable social commitment. But in each of these works, I see many faces, some that do not belong to any space or time but which are still as real and true as any. Because these questions are personal, delicate, private, we are forced to arm ourselves, to don more and more layers of armour. And yet while we do this, under these breastplates and cuirasses, the self is destroyed.

We should no longer believe that it is our duty to

live in the shadow of our husbands and endure, with our magnificence of spirit and our ability to sacrifice, whatever is meted out to us.

My dream: that the much-vaunted patience and endurance of my nation's women should die as quick and clean a death as possible.

~

A memory that I did not want to put down. Or was I simply trying to avoid it? But when I have told so much so freely, why avoid this one? To do injustice to myself? Namdeo's father became more and more of a problem. He loved stale rice fried in oil—shilabhaat we call it. But when I gave it to him, he would tell Namdeo, 'Your wife gives me left-overs.' There were many other minor irritations, all compounded by the fact that he was now hard of hearing. And whether I spoke about him or not, he felt I was speaking about him.

One day, our neighbour, Jainu, had a son. Namdeo told his father the news happily: 'They have a son.'

'Chhah? Rubbish. Not one?'

We couldn't help laughing.

At most times he was okay, but there were times when he was difficult. But I would make excuses for him, telling myself he was an old man with only one son, where else could he go? And so I held my peace.

But then an unexpected thing happened.

I began to experience sleep disturbances. I would get up screaming in the night. I would feel an intense pressure on my entire body, on my veins, blood, muscles, everything was as if dead. I would be so filled with fear that I couldn't scream, couldn't lift a finger. This state would last a couple of minutes and then I would get up, screaming. This happened again and again. It had never happened before and I suspect it was because of all the talk of separation and all the fights. I went to Dr Patkar. He prescribed some pills but those left me sleepy all day. I could only manage to eat and sleep.

One day, I served Namdeo's father and went to sleep. Later, he began to vomit and started saying that I had poisoned him. I woke with a start and was filled with rage. What did these people think of themselves? Were they so rich and so important that I might want to kill them? For what? Their estates and wealth?

Namdeo took his father's side. But then this began to happen again. Namdeo took him for a check-up and they took an X-ray of his stomach. It was a stomach problem—the beginnings of one. The doctor advised him to give up tobacco which was causing him to vomit. The old man refused to believe him. He preferred to blame me. That was when I opened my mouth.

'I did not come to your door, begging for your protection. If you're afraid I'm going to poison you, don't stay here. Go build yourself a bungalow and live in it.

Actually, I should be the one accusing you of poisoning me and ruining my health. If I die, you get the house. What do I get out of killing you? Stones and mud?'

I just didn't care. From that moment on, I stopped bothering about my in-laws and the rest of Namdeo's family. Whether they were there or not mattered nothing to me now.

Namdeo was very fond of his father. As for his mother, though she had seen some terrible times, he said what he wanted to her. Once or twice he even struck her. The poor woman would break down and be reduced to a sobbing mess. But the next day, she'd be back, looking after him again.

This made me angry. I would tell him about this and he would use bad language, sarcasm, every device of pain, and then he would be speaking sweetly again. He would touch his feet and hug her and all that nonsense. However sincere these apologies were, what he did was unforgivable. His rough behaviour caused everyone grief. But they were all too scared to do anything about it.

~

During the first year of marriage, a friend of mine told me to apply for a clerical job at the Reserve Bank of India. I did so. I was told there was only a nominal examination to be passed. My English was not very good but my friend said, 'Just give the paper and leave the rest to me.' But when I went there, I discovered that this was a job that was reserved for the Scheduled Caste-Scheduled Tribe candidates. My principles would not allow this.

'I'm not a Mahar. I'm not a Brahmin either. I don't believe in caste. How can I apply for a job that is reserved on the basis of caste?'

'Listen, it's only an application you have to write. It's just a process they have.'

This did not sit well with my principles. Today, I marry a Mahar, I became a Mahar? Tomorrow I marry a Brahmin, I become a Brahmin? Do I have any independent existence of my own if it changes with my marriage?

I never went back.

My husband's name—how can that be my name?

My husband's achievements—how can those be my achievements?

~

Before my marriage, there was a Muslim family that lived across from us. The head of the house was never at home. He was the owner of seven or eight factories. This was his fourth wife from whom he had two girls and two boys. Twice a month, he would hobble up on his cane. Even as he got out of his car, he would be looking at the women passing up and down the street. When no one was around, I would go over and meet my friend, Siraj.

She was the youngest child and exquisite, the kind to be wrapped up in a burkha for her own good. Her father was an old man; her mother a young woman who loved the good life. She liked eating paan, playing cards and getting dressed up and going to the pictures. When Siraj came of age, she became even lovelier, big-breasted, a girl of ferocious beauty. And yet on her face there was the shine of innocence.

No one went to the beauty parlour in those days but she had no need: her rainbow-shaped brows, those long lashes, those almond eyes were all gifts of nature.

The entire neighbourhood was mad about her. There was a boy on the floor above whom she liked too and he began to make fifty or sixty trips a day just to see her. He would serenade her too. When her mother found out, she was forbidden from going out. She wouldn't even let Siraj go to the toilet. Then her aged father died of a heart attack and suddenly the wonderful life of paan and pictures came to an abrupt end.

Finally, she sold the priceless gem of her daughter's beauty to an Arab. I have noticed one thing about Muslim women: they are unequalled in their beauty. But they're firmly blinkered by religion. They seem to be numb, insensitive. Year after year is spent in seeing films, in entertainment, in eating and having fun. Some of them do not even know this life. The men take great care that their women should not be exposed to the dangerous winds of freedom. I often wondered why there had been no social reformer to challenge this tradition.

~

'Dalit' means 'exploited', 'oppressed', they say. Today this word is used by many people to describe only the Mahar, the Mang, the Chambhar, the Vimukta, and the bhatkya (nomadic tribes). But how these people view the women of their own communities is also interesting.

A worker called Prakash Ramteke came to us from Nagpur. He was one of a group who had raised their voices against Namdeo there. But still Namdeo brought him to stay with us. He was treated well, good food was cooked for him, he was given gifts. He would also, in turn, help with the housework.

He would fetch the laundry and buy cigarettes, or vegetables and milk. He would drop Ashu to school. He stayed with us for two years. During his time at Saat Rasta, he seduced a young woman. She was a bit of an innocent, ignorant, someone who did not leave the house much. He was twenty-five years old, a graduate and had a bit of political awareness and some ideas of his own. When things began to accelerate between them, I got to know about the affair. I caught them in time. They were ready to elope. When Namdeo brought them back, Ramteke admitted to the affair. He said he was ready to marry her. Everyone approved of this. Jilebis were distributed. He even brought some relatives from Nagpur to see the girl. Actually, Prakash was Raja Dhale's supporter and follower. But he stayed with us. After that someone made some mischief and he did not show up, leaving the girl high and dry.

One day, Raja Dhale came over. I told him what had happened. He refused to acknowledge any responsibility for the man.

'But why does Namdeo entertain such workers?' he asked.

'I wish I knew,' I said. 'But what is to become of the girl? Look at how he fooled us.'

Raja Dhale laughed. 'What are you talking about?' he asked. 'He's well educated. How would such an unlettered bride suit him?'

And then I remembered: when I was getting married and my family had protested saying that I had to finish my education, this very Raja Dhale had said, 'What does your family want? Security? Who can give you an assurance of security, right up to the end?'

When it was about me, security was not an issue because his friend was in a hurry to become my husband. But when it was his worker, he wanted him to have the security of an educated wife. Nice.

I saw many people from the Dalit community at close quarters. I was aloof and detached. I had one advantage.

Because I had not been brought up with any caste or

religious influences, because my family had not observed the rites and rituals of any faith, I could observe them all in a dispassionate manner.

The man-woman relationship in the entire community seemed to be terribly unjust and unfair to women. Every man seemed to have two or three wives and a mistress on the side. Many had abandoned their first wives for one reason or the other.

~

One of Namdeo's distant relations had courted and won a Muslim girl and even married her on the quiet. This was done in cinematic style, with the exchange of garlands in a temple. Her mother threatened to have him beaten up. She offered him money too. She went to the police and complained that her daughter was under-age and that the boy had abducted her. He brought the affair to Namdeo. They were a proper Laila-Majnoon pair. They were both arrested. She could not bear the pangs of parting and spent her days in tears. Everyone was rather surprised at their being in love. She was an innocent, with dreamy eyes, a true Muslim beauty. His was the face of a vessel left unwashed for many days. Finally, she was allowed to go and live with him. The marriage did not last; they got divorced after a year.

~

Namdeo's father had married twice. And then there were his other affairs. But the odd thing was that this did not seem to worry either of his wives very much.

~

Namdeo had a smart, well-educated friend, an excise officer. His wife came from the village and, of course, she had to stay with us. The woman was illiterate, odd to look at, and there seemed to be something abnormal about her face. She had an infant in her arms when she arrived, wrapped in a tattered cloth. She said the child was about a year old but he was the size of a newborn. He could not even hold his head up. There was something not quite right about him too. He looked ill, as if he were about to die.

His limbs were matchsticks, his face contorted. She had brought this sickly child all the way to Mumbai and now she took him out into the heat of the sun as she wandered around the city. But none of this surprised me as much as the excise officer's behaviour. He neither came to the house nor did he see her.

Later he accused her of doing black magic and divorced her. He claimed the child and married another woman.

~

Another of Namdeo's associates from the first stage of the Dalit Movement had grown so absorbed in the revolution that his wife had run away with another revolutionary. He would get drunk and under the influence, he would advise Namdeo: 'Don't harass your wife too much. Take care of her,' he would say with malicious earnestness, as if deeply concerned about my welfare.

~

Another of his friends was always drunk, night and day. And yet he wrote beautiful literary speeches. He would go and sign the muster at his workplace and turn around and come right home. He had a career as a writer and was known for his boldness. He was married with a wife and a child but he also had another woman whom he had set up in the same chawl. His wife found out and shamed him in front of everyone. This curtailed his amorous activities for a while but then he was back with the other woman again.

After the usual fights and beatings, his wife grew tired of this and left him and came to me. I, of course, would take the woman's side and fight on her behalf. At the time Namdeo was in hospital. I let her stay with me. I would take her husband to task about his drinking. He was scared of me. He held this against me. What he could not understand was how the same woman who showed such contempt for him could show such respect for his wife. When his wife came to live with me, I reassured her, 'Take this to be your mother's home. You can stay as long as you like.'

I tried my best to find her a job too. But it did not work. In a few days, she was a broken woman, pining for her child. Then Namdeo's aunt told her off.

'That is your home by right. Why have you left it and come here? Give it to him left and right; he deserves it. But it does not become you to come here and leave your child.' And so on.

That did it. The woman marched off home. Her husband was there, drunk as a skunk. She took whatever came to hand—slippers, brooms—and began to beat him. She released all her pent-up rage that day. The next day, her husband began to suffer from a form of alcohol-induced madness. He was delirious. Finally, the neighbours got together and tied him up and took him to the mental hospital.

When he recovered and came back, he started telling everyone: 'Namdeo took my wife and set her up in his own home.'

~

There was an intelligent Dalit boy who worked in a bank. He would also try and write. His addiction became so severe that he would blow up his entire salary on alcohol. His wife also had a job. They had a sweet child.

For a while, he pulled himself together. He got a job in Air India. But then he slipped again and the whole sorry story played itself out. Finally he began to drink so much, he would fall into gutters. He would come over like this which would annoy me immensely. He would have only his trousers and banian on; his shirt he would have pawned for booze money. And in this condition he would come to ask Namdeo for money.

~

All these tragedies can be traced back to addictions which seemed to happen where there was no direction and no purpose to life. The movement's alcoholic tragedies, its despairs, the corrupt and lecherous behaviour of the leaders, the sell-outs, these were all reasons. Otherwise, where most men find it difficult to maintain one wife, how do these men manage with three wives? It isn't just a question of being sexually dissatisfied. It is the only way left to demonstrate their masculinity.

Two or three times Namdeo was called upon to arbitrate in marital disputes. I would say acerbically, 'What a funny old world we live in. We ask the unjust to dole out justice. And if that isn't funny, what is?'

But truly, how can a woman hope for justice? How can a man who has never tried to understand her side of things, who has no respect for her rights or her independence, ever hope to ensure justice for her as a woman?

~

The world of men fills me with curiosity...and jealousy. How different their world is. They can live anywhere, they can go anywhere. And regardless of what they have done, in their declining years, they command respect and good will from the community.

The pleasures of a cigarette, the high of a peg of alcohol, ganja, bhang, opium, charas, Laal Pari. What could these be like? What kind of happiness would be found in each one?

And to have sex with a prostitute? While enjoying these women, do they ever think of their wives sitting alone at home, waiting for them?

Where is a woman's real place in today's society? Is she aware of all that is happening around her? And what are her ways out of it? I accept that all these are intensely personal questions. But no one wishes to pay attention to them. What does a woman have with which to fight injustice? Must she continue to be sacrificed like this? Whatever traditions have been dismantled, have only freed men. I won't even go into what I've gained from telling you my sob story.

I am now of the firm opinion that women must exploit their own husbands. Yes. I agree that this is an extreme and foolish remark but I mean it in a polemical way. But what else am I to say when confronted with the image of an Aryan woman who is burned alive by her mother-in-law and husband; who counts herself lucky if she is allowed to endure her husband's infidelities and violence?

~

A little about Namdeo's father's sister, his aunt. She was an extraordinary and exceptional woman. When she was a child, she would exercise with a lathi. The maids in the house would run away, afraid of that whirling stick. No one had the guts to take her on. She was very rich and that gave her considerable clout. But this was more than literal. She would haul her daughters-in-law up when she was annoyed with them and bang them on the ground. Namdeo's mother had also been treated in this manner.

Namdeo's uncle's wife was something else again.

This was a memory of her childhood. She had been married off very young, still at the age when panties and a blouse was enough clothing. Her husband was a young man. He would dress her up and set her on his shoulders and roam about. I had no idea whether this story made me want to laugh or cry.

Atyabai's story. Her mother-in-law was a widow. She was still a young woman. Her son was in Mumbai, working. And playing in the house was a little girl, her daughter-in-law, young enough to be her daughter. And so the mother-in-law gave in to temptation. Their house was outside the village so she could conduct this affair away from prying eyes. Then one day, the mother-in-law's stomach began to hurt. It wouldn't stop and her daughter-in-law had no idea what to do. She refused to let the little one call anyone either. The midwife arrived and made the little girl stand outside the house.

In a little while, it was all done. The midwife went off into the sunset carrying a bundle with some undisclosed thing inside it.

'What's happened to you?' the little girl asked her mother-in-law.

'Don't tell anyone or I'll beat you. There was a worm in my tummy. That was removed. Now I'm feeling better. Go now. Go and wash my clothes in the river.'

The little girl looked out. It was dark.

'So late in the night?'

'Why? Who's going to eat you up? If you wash the clothes in the morning, the women will ask questions. Go now.'

Quaking and quivering, the little girl took the bundle of bloody clothing to the river and began to wash them. This took a while and then she had to come home with the clean bundle. Naturally, she was up late the next morning and when she got to the river, the other women were already hard at work.

'So late?' they asked.

'Slept late,' she said.

'Why?'

'My mum-in-law's tummy was really hurting.'

'So what did you do?'

'She sent me, didn't she? To wash the clothes in the night?'

The women began to cluck and coo: 'What was she thinking?' 'Fancy sending a poor little girl, out in the middle of the night.' 'And to the river, at that!'

The little girl opened up to the sympathy.

'See, she had this worm in her tummy, no? And that had to be taken out and there was lots of blood. So she told me to take her clothes and wash them there. She said I wasn't to tell anyone so don't tell her I told you, please?'

The cat was out of the bag. Naturally everyone in the village got to know the facts in the case. The mother-in-law was left with no place to hide her face and she beat the little girl with the handle of an axe.

When I heard the story I was stunned but Namdeo's auntie laughed softly behind the edge of her sari.

~

In truth, what do I have today? I sometimes feel afraid of my own militancy. What do I really want? What is it that keeps me fighting although I have no weapons in my armoury? Where did this rebellion come from? Why could I not erase my self, my personality, and sacrifice myself?

This rebellion, this existential angst, this suffering, how long will it last? What do I want?

I no longer want to pour my life into singing. I tried to immerse myself in colour and form. I no longer feel like picking up the brushes. I often wonder if there is an area of endeavour in which I can lose myself. This seems to have been the reason why I have struggled.

When I see Smita Patil on the screen, a sharp pain surges into my heart. I could have been there, I think, where she is. She brought to life the roles I would have loved to do. They were my roles, I feel, by rights. As I watch one of her films, her face fades away and mine superimposes itself. Then I become aware of the huge gap between reality and my dreams. The same thing happens when I hear Gulzar's songs and dialogue.

Everything seems so close and so far, all at once.

So where will I find fulfilment?

Did I want to be an actor for fame? For money? For glamour? You could say these were secondary reasons for wanting a career in the performing arts. But more than all these, it was for the complete fulfilment of creation. The bliss of creating something new. I wanted that extraordinary high.

I had experienced the joy of being applauded, the high of putting make-up on, that incomparable intoxication of slipping into another persona, the familiar smell of the green room. That was the world I wanted to belong to.

'Kaahe tarsaaye jeeyara' (Why does my heart mock me?) and other songs by Asha Bhosale set my feet tapping, my body vibrating, my head nodding. Then I see reality around me, the people, the noise, the discussions, the poetry, Namdeo the hero of it all and I feel crucified, aloof, and lifeless. This is like a game of hide-and-seek that I play with myself even as I try to understand myself.

~

Once again Vincent Van Gogh comes to mind. This is like a wound that never heals. I am ashamed of myself. Why could I not throw it all away as this man had? Why did I console myself in this narrow frame, eating the bread of the abject? For my husband's bed? How many desires one has submitted to, carrying this femininity as one bears a boil.

I have often tried to assess myself. I have dragged my life into the dust. I have pulled myself down to the lowest rung of the ladder. That hurts me. I was proud of myself. I did have self-respect. But it was my opinion—and still is—that every woman is born free and should seek to keep that freedom at any cost. As long as a woman makes her husband and her home the top priority in her life, she is bound to suffer. As of now, it is the extent to which a woman sacrifices herself to her husband's needs and wants that earns her a position of respect in society. But which man, or which person, will ever willingly relinquish power? Eventually it is the male ego that we women nurture. No woman should ever tolerate deception. This is the most demeaning thing for her. Do women have physical needs? When a man expects loyalty and love from his wife, should he not offer her the same commitment? Extramarital affairs are common things, people say, and dismiss them. Because men rule. They will justify any behaviour that is to their benefit.

But women are also complicit with their narrow-minded thinking and their silences. 'Men are like that. Eventually, he will come back home,' they say, unwilling to show the world how badly they are being treated. No woman benefits from this silence for as much as she bears, more will be heaped upon her.

~

I feel I have to add one more thing. I hope this autobiography is not just the story of the quarrels between a husband and wife. And I hope it does not seem as if I have offered a one-sided view of things, my side. Truly, I was fighting against the system of male domination. Namdeo was not a villain in that fight. Every person is at one time or the other, a villain. Not just Namdeo, the social system in which we live was also responsible for what I had to suffer.

I still love Namdeo's poetry. I still love Namdeo, the poet. Because Namdeo Dhasal is still honest in his poetry. But it is one thing to fall in love and quite another thing to love. I have fallen short there and this may be my failure from his point of view. But I doubt that a good poet can make a good husband or partner.

~

Once Ashu said, 'I'm going to marry Mummy.'

Both of us laughed. We explained that no one marries his mother.

'Then I'll get Mummy married to someone else,' he said next.

Neither of us knew what to say.

I was the only woman Ashu knew of, the only role model for womanhood. He would go to bed when I told him to so that I would not get angry. If I fell ill, he would fuss around me, trying to do whatever he could. He liked only people he could see I liked. So I had to be very careful about how I spoke and behaved or Namdeo would accuse me of filling him with Brahminical culture.

I would say, 'I have no problem if he ends up filled with Brahmin culture. But I don't want him to absorb any of your traits. I don't want him abusing people and trying to push them around. I don't mind if my son ends up with middle-class values. Instead of being a corrupt revolutionary, I wouldn't mind him aspiring to the higher middle class. I want my child to be happy and cultured.'

~

Ashu and I had a good relationship. I would suggest new games and buy him new toys. He would often forget I was his mother.

~

One day Namdeo beat me mercilessly. Ashu began to cry. Namdeo took a slipper and hit me on the back. I screamed in pain. I nearly fainted. I banged my head and feet on the floor, I felt suffocated. Then Ashu threw his small body on the floor. He began to shriek and thrash about.

Namdeo's rage came to an abrupt end. He ran to his son and picked him up. He tried to calm him down, to pat him, but Ashu's screams would not cease. In a voice that was close to tears, Namdeo said to me, 'See what's wrong with him. Do something please. He may die.'

He grabbed me and held me tight.

I was tense, tired and in pain. I felt myself beginning to lose consciousness. I clawed my way back and when I came to, I was still trembling. Namdeo was terrified now.

I held Ashu close and went to sleep.

The next day, Ashu asked, 'A chappal hurts, no? Did it hurt much?'

My heart ached. Had I brought this moment on my son? Which child should have to ask such a question? What could I say? I just swallowed my feelings and was silent.

Then he said, 'If I were a big man, I would have beaten Dada to a pulp.'

Inside, I felt a bitter happiness well up.

Each time he beat me, Namdeo would spend the next two days in a state of repentance. He would try and explain. He would hug me and kiss me. He would feed me with his own hands. He would praise me immoderately. But my hurts remained raw and my wounded dreams would not heal.

~

So what next? Where do the roads lead from here? What tests await me? Should I live alone? Should I slip away? Living in the shadow of this man will stunt me. Somewhere all this must end. I cannot sacrifice my selfhood, my individuality on the altar of Namdeo Dhasal's authoritarian despotic personality. Why do I behave so helpless? After he has beaten me, cheated on me, abused me, how can I go back to his embrace, how can I talk to him? Perhaps I really loved him? But was I to suffer this love to the end? I wanted his support. I would run to embrace him in a vulnerable state. I didn't want him to be a husband then. I just wanted to snuggle up to him, to hide my face in him, to become a child again and to mock him gently. (I still do.) I would tie up my hair in two childlike plaits and demand chocolate from him. He would say proudly, 'Sometimes, she seems to be a girl. I feel like I have married a doll.'

After all these experiences, there is still something of the child left alive in me.

When I was a girl, it was as if happiness followed me around, begging for a smile while I looked on grim and serious. And today in the middle of the bitter reality, my childhood still surges, like a fountain.

~

This then is my little story so far.

'You're writing your autobiography? Now?' someone asked.

'Does experience ask for your age before it happens to you? Must one be a certain age before one sits down to write? Isn't depth a better measure of life than length?'

What I am going to achieve now, I do not know. At the most, I suppose I will feel the pressure of malicious curiosity. Those who are close to me might get angry or feel hurt. But I have unburdened myself.

Sometimes I think it might have been best to keep this hidden, to crush the poisonous butterfly inside my fist, to stop it from fluttering. But being aware can be disturbing. Perhaps if I had remained wilfully ignorant and lived according to tradition, things might have ended differently. I might have been happy. In the end, do I need to wear the shirt of the happy man? Who is to engineer the jail break that women must make to attain self-hood, independence? I am just one more face in a mass of ignored faceless women. I hope this book will help at least one woman find her face, that it might help her find her way out of her circumscribed and stuffy world. For this one woman's sake, I am willing to bear whatever criticism patriarchal society heaps upon me.

My life has not been an outstanding one. There's no ladder of success. Nor does it have to show a rising graph of success. It isn't as if I've suffered much either. This is the story of a straightforward woman, any young woman. No colours have been added but I hope that like a kaleidoscope it will reveal new patterns to each new viewer.

~

This is the story of a defeat, a lonely defeat. In the time I have been speaking to all of you, I could put down my mask for a while. That's all…